UNDERCOVER

The Library of Espionage and Secret Warfare

CRESCENT BOOKS

UNDERCOVER

Codes and Ciphers

Peter Way

W.R.N.S. Cypher Office Naval C-in-C's H.Q.

Editorial Consultant:
ERIC CLARK
Series Coordinator: John Mason
Picture Editor: Peter Cook
Designer: Ann Dunn
Editor: Mitzi Bales
Copy Editor: Maureen Cartwright
Research: Patricia Mandel
General Consultant: Beppie Harrison

Crescent Books
A Division of Crown Publishers, Inc.
a b c d e f g h
ISBN 0-517-218674
Library of Congress Catalog
Card No. 76-55553
© 1977 Aldus Books Limited
First published in the United Kingdom
in 1977 by Aldus Books Limited
D. L.: S. S. 730 - 76
Printed and bound in Spain
by TONSA San Sebastián
and RONER Madrid

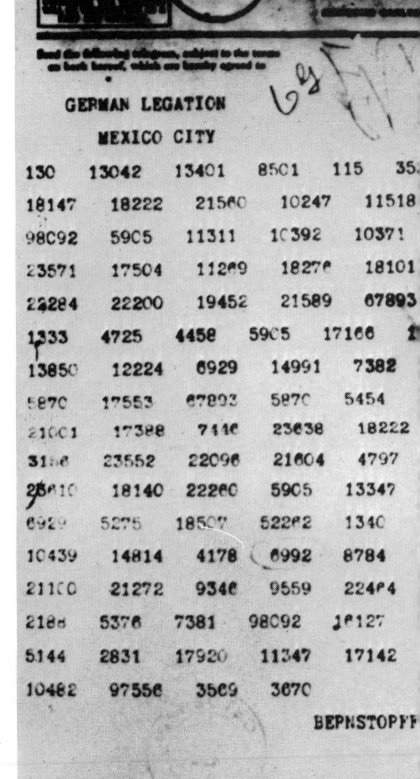

Messages in secret writing have been the backbone of espionage and undercover activities for thousands of years — and modern technology has made cryptology more of a brain teaser than ever. How do codes and ciphers work, and how are they broken? This book explains the encoding and decoding of messages in a clear way, and also recounts some of the most exciting stories in espionage history to point up how codes and ciphers have directly affected events. Among the classic tales are the Zimmermann telegram, the PURPLE machine, and ULTRA.

Contents

Left: part of the Zimmermann telegram. Decoding of this message, in which Germany offered Mexico part of the United States in return for her cooperation, pushed the USA into World War I.

Frontispiece: a painting of the Wrens' (Women's Royal Naval Service) cipher office at the Naval Commander-in-Chief's Headquarters in 1944.

Why Codes and Ciphers?

1

The Spartan general read the letter that the slave had brought him, then tossed it aside. Its contents were relatively unimportant, and it was not too surprising that the hostile forces that stood between Sparta and General Lysander's camp had allowed the slave to pass through their lines and complete his harmless mission. But the general's eye spotted something his enemies had ignored. After dismissing his attendants, he turned to the slave and demanded: "Give me your belt."

The slave complied. It was an ordinary leather belt, except for one detail. Around it, seemingly as a decoration, ran a series of letters. They made no sense.

Lysander carefully wound the belt in a spiral around a baton. Now the letters were no longer a mere jumble; along the length of the baton they fell into rows of meaningful words. The words conveyed bad news—that the Persians, supposedly Sparta's allies, were planning to take over the state. Armed with this knowledge, Lysander rushed his troops back to Sparta and crushed the plot.

Lysander's deciphering the message on the slave's belt is one of the earliest recorded examples of what has today become a highly sophisticated business: cryptology. The simple Spartan device, called a *scytale* (rhymes with Italy), has long since been surpassed by complex electronic machines and codes and ciphers of mind-cracking complexity. Nor is code-breaking any longer the direct concern of generals; instead, the generals have at their service small armies of cryptographers (those who devise the methods of sending secret messages) and cryptanalysts (those who puzzle out the other side's secret messages).

Located outside Washington D.C. is the headquarters of the National Security Agency, the major cryptological organization in the U.S. government. Within this vast building, constructed in the late 1950s at a cost of $35 million, work some 14,000 people. Another 2000 work in the agency's outposts throughout the world. The U.S. Army, Navy, and Air Force have their own cryptologic agencies, which operate under the guidance of the NSA. Other government agencies, under the jurisdiction of the Departments of State and of Justice (for example, the FBI), are also concerned with cryptology. By 1966 the cost of running

Above: an ancient Greek vase showing Greek soldiers in battle. The Spartans were the most warlike of the Greeks. They devised the earliest system of military cryptography, which on several occasions enabled them to get the better of their adversaries.

Left: the Spartan general Lysander as portrayed in an engraving of the 18th century.

the NSA alone was reported to be around $1000 million—more than $15 a year from each American taxpayer. Among the agency's costly activities is the launching of satellites to intercept messages sent by other nations' electronic communications media. The science of codes and ciphers has come a long way since Lysander read the message on the slave's belt simply by winding it around a baton.

Yet however complex and expensive code-making and code-breaking have become, they remain in some basic respects unchanged. We still have two main ways of concealing a message. One of these is *steganography*, in which the existence of the message is concealed; the microdot is an example of this kind of concealment. The other way is *cryptography*, in which the message, or "plaintext," is transformed in some way. It may be transformed by substituting one set of letters, numbers, or symbols for the letters of the plaintext. Or it may be done by

Below: the *scytale,* earliest piece of apparatus devised for use in cryptology. Invented by the Spartans, it is probably one of the only known devices for encoding and decoding transposition ciphers. The message is hidden among letters written on paper that has been wrapped around a wooden rod, and seems to be a strip of paper containing letters at random (left). When rewrapped on a rod of the same size, however, the letters align to make complete sense (right).

transposing the letters, as in an anagram. For example, *range* can be transposed into ANGER, or—more confusingly—into a nonsense group of letters, such as AEGNR.

Although the word "code" is commonly used to refer to all systems of cryptography, it is properly used only for systems in which words or syllables are the plaintext units to be converted; systems in which individual letters are the units converted are called ciphers. In modern cryptography, one system is often used on top of another: a code may be enciphered and the resulting nonsensical groups of letters transposed to confuse further the cryptanalysts on the other side.

We often encounter codes in ordinary life. The innocent-looking numbers on your credit card may reveal, to those equipped to understand them, more than you might care to have known about your financial reliability. In packaging foods, manufacturers sometimes put into code the date on which the product will be unfit for sale: shopkeepers know the code, but customers do not. Tramps and vagabonds have their own code indicating the type of welcome one may receive at a house, and scratch the appropriate symbol on the gatepost or on a tree trunk as a signal to their fellows. Art and antique dealers have private languages. When an art dealer designates a painting as a "Rubens" in a sales catalogue only the uninitiated will assume it is by the master himself; dealers and experienced buyers know that according to the code only a "Peter Paul Rubens" is authentic: a "Rubens" is a painting from his school or one merely attributed to the Flemish master.

The degree of secrecy in such codes is obviously very slight. Although only a small percentage of the population may know the code, an outsider could "crack" it with relative ease. By contrast, in the world of military and diplomatic intelligence, the secrecy of a code is of paramount importance. Keeping the code secret may be literally a matter of life and death. The same applies to the tedious and sometimes dangerous business of breaking the code of one's opponents. The very process of analyzing a code must be conducted in the utmost secrecy. While the generals get the headlines—and later the medals—the silent army of cryptanalysts provides them with the information that often makes their triumphs possible. The risks this work may entail—not to mention the mental strain cryptanalysts undergo—remain for the most part unknown to the public.

Sheer physical courage is often demanded of those who work in what has been dubbed "practical cryptanalysis"—that is, stealing the other side's codes. During World War I a young diving instructor, E. C. Miller, recovered many of the Germans' code books from U-boats sunk in the English Channel. Time and again Miller would descend through the cold black water into the wrecked hull of a German ship and make his way through the debris and the corpses of its crew. He also had live companions during his labors. "I found scores of conger eels," he reported, "some of them seven to eight feet long and five

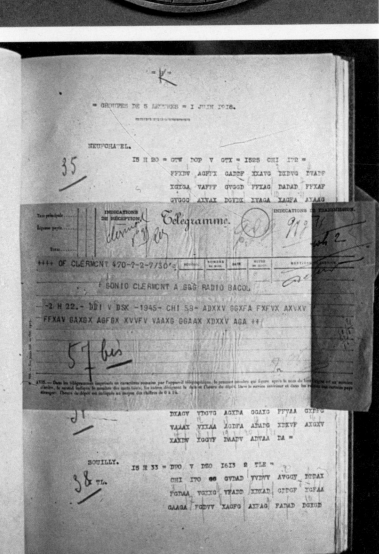

Above: this seemingly innocent sketch hides a simple message consisting of "Ypres 8th." The collar and tie form a Y; the pipe P; the legs and body R; the right hand E; the nose S; the head and cap form 8; and the smoke TH.

Above left: Bolton's Cipher Wheel, a 19th-century version of the cipher disk invented in the 15th century by Leon Battista Alberti, a man of many talents. The inner wheel is moved to place a prearranged index letter against a letter of the outer wheel, that letter becoming the first one of the cipher text. After three or four words, the index letter is moved to another outside letter, changing the encipherment completely. An identical wheel is used for decoding. This mechanical device speeded up the process of cryptology.

Left: a coded message sent by the Germans in World War I in their ADFGVX cipher. With it is a page of workings by Georges Painvin, the brilliant French cryptanalyst who solved it. The complexity of codes in this century put code-breakers under great strain mentally and physically. Painvin lost 33 pounds in his efforts to solve the ingenious ADFGVX cipher, and had to spend six months in the hospital before he fully recovered.

9

inches or so thick, all busily feeding. They gave one a bit of a shock." Almost always, he succeeded in finding the iron box containing the current code. His finds helped the British cryptanalysis department, Room 40, to decipher some 15,000 secret German communications.

The Codes of Zeppelin L-49

Another kind of courage sometimes required in the code-breaking game is that of persisting against apparently hopeless odds. The story of Zeppelin L-49, also from World War I, is an example of this dogged kind of courage.

Returning to the German-occupied zone of France after a bombing raid on London, the zeppelin was quickly losing altitude. The last of its fuel had gone during the night as its propellers churned ineffectually against a violent headwind

Below: this painting shows English divers searching in the wreckage of a German submarine for the black box containing its naval codes. Recovery of an enemy's code and cipher books by whatever means available is often called "practical cryptanalysis."

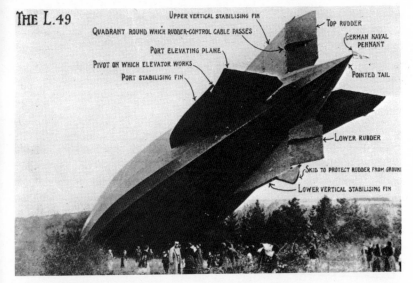

THE L.49

UPPER VERTICAL STABILISING FIN
QUADRANT ROUND WHICH RUDDER-CONTROL CABLE PASSES
PORT ELEVATING PLANE
PIVOT ON WHICH ELEVATOR WORKS
PORT STABILISING FIN
TOP RUDDER
GERMAN NAVAL PENNANT
POINTED TAIL
LOWER RUDDER
SKID TO PROTECT RUDDER FROM GROUND
LOWER VERTICAL STABILISING FIN

Left: the German airship L-49 after being forced to land in France. Before landing, its captain had ordered its code books shredded and scattered through the forest below them. U.S. Army Intelligence managed to recover most of the scraps and gain some useful information from them.

over the English Channel. The captain had had no choice but to continue. If he had allowed the airship to be blown back over England, it would have met a swift and fiery end at the hands of British gunners. Now it was drifting silently, unsteerable as a child's balloon, closer and closer to the treetops of free France— miles from the German zone.

Capture by the Allies was inevitable. But there was one thing that must not be captured under any circumstances: the code books. The captain of a doomed ship can dispose of his secret codes simply by letting them go down with the vessel (on the chance that they will not be retrieved for the enemy by a skilled diver). An army commander can burn his codes. On a hydrogen-filled zeppelin, setting light to the code books is a risky undertaking. The captain briefly considered the measure and then rejected it.

The airship bumped to a landing in front of an astonished rural policeman, and not far from a U.S. Army base. When the Americans entered its cabins they found no trace of the code books or any coded material.

Colonel Richard Williams of U.S. Army Intelligence was not a man to accept defeat. Immediately he ordered his men to retrace on foot the course the zeppelin had taken. It was fortunately well-marked—littered with branches from trees whose tops had been grazed by the descending airship. Scattered among the grass and foliage were thousands of scraps of paper: the crew had spent their last airborne hours in shredding the documents.

By nightfall Williams and his team had 22 sacks full of paper. The task of piecing together the documents was clearly impossible. The word "impossible," however, is not in a cryptanalyst's vocabulary. Williams's men continued working far into the night at their seemingly futile task. Shortly after midnight, another officer, Lieutenant Samuel Hubbard, strolled into the room where they were working. Casually he picked up a fragment no more than an inch wide. A jagged line ran across it, intersected by a web of fine straight lines. At each intersection were sets of letters.

By a near miracle, that jagged line meant something to this particular lieutenant. An avid yachtsman, he recognized the outline of a bay into which, before the war, he had put his boat. Excitedly, the others gathered around him and began the painstaking—but at least possible—task of piecing together a complete map of the North Sea, showing the call sign positions for U-boat rendezvous.

The Yardley Symptom

The kind of courage most often demanded of cryptanalysts is the courage to stretch the mind to its breaking point, the willingness to stick with a problem until it becomes an obsession. Herbert Osborne Yardley, head of the American military intelligence during World War I, once described briefly how a code-breaking problem could dominate one's life. "It was the first thing I thought of when I awakened, the last when I fell asleep." This kind of obsession is known among cryptanalysts as the "Yardley symptom."

A myriad possible solutions, false leads, and algebraic equations dance before the eyes of the code-breaker. The elusive secret seems always to lie around the next corner. He may suffer from nightmares in which he is doomed to search on a beach of pebbles for two stones exactly alike. He may have a nervous breakdown. Or he may remain apparently calm himself but strike a kind of terror into his associates.

One who did so was the Russian cryptanalyst Zybine. This gifted eccentric was once given an unusually difficult cipher by the chief of the Moscow secret police. The year was 1911, and revolutionaries were busy with plots to overthrow the government and assassinate the czar. For hour after hour the sharp-eyed Zybine sat scrutinizing the maze of fractions in which the message was written, scribbling possible solutions on one sheet of paper after another, oblivious to everything except the problem. The police chief had to call him twice to dinner. After the soup course, Zybine turned the dish over and tried to write on the back of it. The pencil wouldn't mark the china, so he wrote on his shirt cuffs. Finally he jumped up exclaiming, "Tishe idiote, dalshe budiote!" The Russian proverb, which means "Who walks softly goes far," was the key to the cipher. After this breakthrough, it was easy to decipher the message.

In the opinion of his friend the police chief, Zybine was "a fanatic, not to say a maniac. . . . Simple ciphers he cleared up at a glance, but complicated ciphers placed him in a state almost of a trance from which he did not emerge until the problem was resolved."

No one knows when man first began to communicate through verbal language, but it must have been not long after that that

Bribery by Code

The presidential election of 1876 between Samuel J. Tilden for the Democrats and Rutherford B. Hayes for the Republicans was the most disputed ballot in the history of the United States. Congress had to appoint a special Electoral Commission to decide which candidate had won, and this commission decided on the Republican by a majority of only one vote. Not until two years later was the full story of the attempted bribery of commission members exposed by newspapers—and the story is one that is hardly ever found in a history book. It might never have been told at all without three amateur code-breakers.

They came into the story during the summer of 1878 when the existence of Democratic coded telegrams was leaked to the New York *Tribune*, an important newspaper with Republican leanings. The leak came from a congressional investigation committee that had been formed under Democratic Party pressure to look into Democratic rumors of Republican efforts to buy electors' votes. The *Tribune* got hold of 27 enciphered telegrams that had been sent by the Democrats.

At first the *Tribune* simply inserted enciphered telegram text in editorials as a way to make the Democrats squirm. But then the public decided to get to the root of the matter by having the texts decoded. Both staff members of the paper and the general public began to try their hand at deciphering.

Meanwhile the Detroit *Post* unearthed a code that had been used by the Democrats in their electoral communications to party members in Oregon during the 1876 campaign. It was a dictionary code previously used for business purposes by J. N. H. Patrick, a successful mine operator who was an important figure in the Democratic Party. The *Post* decoded a telegram that said in part: ". . . Must purchase Republican elector to recognize and act with Democrat and secure vote and prevent trouble. Deposit $10,000 my credit. . . . Answer." The sender was Patrick.

Then the three amateur cryptanalysts, working independently, found keys to the ciphers of other telegrams. One code-breaker was an editor of the *Tribune*, another was the economics writer on it, and the third was a mathematician not connected with the paper. They succeeded around the same time, and the results of their work were made public through the *Tribune*.

The revelations were sensational. One of the telegrams from a close campaign adviser of Tilden, the 1876 Democratic presidential candidate, said that the Democrats could get New York's vote in the electoral college for $200,000. The answering telegram turned down the deal with the words: "Proposition too high." Other telegrams clearly showed that bribery had been attempted in each state whose electoral college votes had been in question. The nephew of the losing Democratic candidate was one of the people implicated, although Tilden himself was cleared of complicity.

The *Tribune* exposé apparently was not forgotten by the public when the next presidential election came up in 1880. The Republicans won again. Was their victory the result of the scandal of the cipher telegrams? At least one writer has said so.

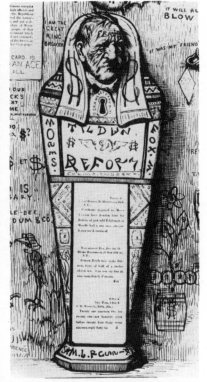

Above: a contemporary cartoon of Democratic candidate Tilden entitled "Cipher Mumm(er)y".

he began to disguise plain language in order to deceive his enemies. And shortly after that someone else must have set himself the task of decoding the secret. Today, secret communications pass back and forth all over the world; corporations signal their intended mergers and takeovers; smugglers alert their accomplices to shipments of illegal guns and drugs; the voices of world leaders talking over the "hot line" are scrambled to prevent comprehension by eavesdroppers.

And as methods of concealment become ever more ingenious, the code-breakers find and develop ingenuity equal to the task. The race has been on for a long time now, and it shows no signs of slackening.

Code Makers, Code Breakers

2

"The black chamber, bolted, hidden, guarded, sees all, hears all." This melodramatic image is not drawn from some history of Renaissance Italy, or from a Gothic novel. It refers to 20th-century America—specifically to a group of cryptanalysts ensconced in a New York City brownstone house just after World War I, ferreting out the secrets of foreign governments. The description was penned by the man who directed their work, Herbert Osborne Yardley. His black chamber, the first American venture into full-time cryptanalysis, followed a long history of such clandestine bureaus.

Behind the activities of kings and generals, popes and presidents, the diligent historian can often find evidence of the black chambers, busily making and breaking secrets for their masters. He will also find extraordinary and brilliant individuals who have furthered the development of cryptography.

For example, the German Benedictine abbot Johannes Trithemius had several highly acclaimed histories and biographies to his credit before he wrote his controversial *Steganographia*, ("covered writing") in 1499. Although it contained some simple codes and ciphers, the book also dealt at some length with telepathy, magic, and other occult matters. For more than 100 years the *Steganographia* was passed around in manuscript form and secretly copied by students of the occult. Not until 1606 was it printed, and shortly afterward it was placed on the Index of Prohibited Books by the Roman Catholic Church. Even in Trithemius's lifetime, however, the book got its author into trouble. The monks of Spanheim, where he was abbot, mutinied and had him removed.

Trithemius managed to find another niche for himself in the monastery of St Jacob in Würzburg; and while prior there he wrote another book, dealing with cryptology alone. Entitled *Polygraphia*, it was published two years after his death in 1516. Its several volumes contained hundreds of alphabets in which words and phrases could be substituted for the individual letters. The most famous of these is the Ave Maria cipher. This massive system consists of 384 columns of Latin words, from which equivalents can be selected in such a way that the plaintext message can be disguised as a harmless piece of devotional

14

POLYGRAPHIAE

LIBRI SEX, IOANNIS TRITHEMII AB
BATIS PEAPOLITANI, QVONDAM
SPANHEIMENSIS, AD MAXI/
MILIANVM CAESAREM.

Cum gratia et priuilegio L. Œ.

·IO. TRITHEMIVS·

A	Jesus	Eternal
B	God	Perpetual
C	Saviour	Infinite
D	King	Angelic
E	Pastor	Immortal
F	Author	Enduring
G	Redemptor	Incomprehensible
H	Prince	Incorruptible
I, J	Maker	Durable
K	Conservator	Permanent
L	Governor	Ineffable
M	Emperor	Celestial
N	Moderator	Divine
O	Rector	Interminable
P	Judge	Perfect
Q	Illustrator	Sincere
R	Illuminator	Pure
S	Consolator	Glorious
T	Sire	Supernatural
U, V, W	Dominator	Indicible
X	Creator	Peaceful
Y	Psalmist	Happy
Z	Sovereign	Excellent
&	Protector	Uplifting

Right: an English translation of two of the code alphabets from Trithemius's *Polygraphia*. Substitution of the words for the plaintext letters concealed the message in somewhat lengthy devotional prose.

Below right: the first few and last few rows of Trithemius's *tabula recta*, or square table, of cipher alphabets. Trithemius was the first to arrange polyalphabets in table form, so all the cipher alphabets in a given system can be seen at once. Because there can be only as many rows as there are letters in the basic alphabet, the table is a square composed of 24 rows. To encode the word HELP by this system, the H—which as the first letter must come from the first alphabet—remains the same. The E must come from the second alphabet in the second row, and becomes F; the L from the third alphabet becomes N; and the P from the fourth alphabet becomes S. HELP becomes HFNS. Longer words use more rows of the cipher alphabets.

TRITHEMIUS' TABULA RECTA

```
A B C D E F G H I K L M N O P Q R S T U X Y Z W
B C D E F G H I K L M N O P Q R S T U X Y Z W A
C D E F G H I K L M N O P Q R S T U X Y Z W A B
D E F G H I K L M N O P Q R S T U X Y Z W A B C
. . . . . . . . . . . . . . . . . . . . . . . .
Y Z W A B C D E F G H I K L M N O P Q R S T U X
Z W A B C D E F G H I K L M N O P Q R S T U X Y
W A B C D E F G H I K L M N O P Q R S T U X Y Z
```

writing. For example, the word *bade* might be rendered (in English translation): "God I hail thee ineffable pastor." Obviously, the drawback to the system is its longwindedness—it requires as many words, and sometimes phrases, as there are letters in the message. In some cases, this might produce a piece of writing that by its sheer length might arouse suspicion.

Another of Trithemius' inventions was the square table *(tabula recta)* of polyalphabets (see the diagram above). This could be used as for a substitution cipher in which the first letter of a message was enciphered with the first alphabet, the second with the second, and so on. For example, the word *help* would be enciphered HFNS.

```
CAESAR'S CIPHER


plain:    a b c d e f g h i j k l m n o p q r s t u v w x y z
cipher:  D E F G H I J K L M N O P Q R S T U V W X Y Z A B C


Example: "supply" becomes VXSSOB
```

Left: a modern English version of a cipher invented by Julius Caesar. Today, any cipher that uses a single alphabet in normal sequence is called a Caesar cipher; but the original displaced the letters by three, as shown here. Below: the 14th-century English poet Geoffrey Chaucer, who was also a customs official and amateur astronomer and practiced cryptography. His work *The Equatorie of the Planetis* contains six passages written in cipher.

Although he was the author of the first printed book devoted to cryptology, Trithemius was by no means the world's first expert on the subject. Even in the Middle Ages, when normal written language was a mystery to most people, a few scholars had toyed with codes and ciphers. And long before that period cryptography was known and practiced.

Egyptian hieroglyphic writing sometimes incorporated a kind of secret writing. Scribes would occasionally employ unusual forms of particular hieroglyphs in place of the more common ones. This was probably an attempt to make the passer-by take a greater interest in the inscription, rather than to discourage him. They only puzzled later generations after the original language had been forgotten.

The earliest known attempt to hide the meaning of written words was discovered in Mesopotamia. A small tablet dating from 1500 B.C. and inscribed with cuneiform figures gives details of how to make certain pottery glazes. It was written at a time when such secrets were jealously guarded. The writer used the correct forms for the various syllables, but the way he juxtaposed them obscured the words themselves. The effect might be loosely compared to George Bernard Shaw's facetious spelling of the word *fish*: GHOTI (the GH of *tough,* the O of *women,* and the TI of *nation*).

The military leaders of ancient times used simple forms of secret writing, the best-known being Julius Caesar's substitution cipher that bears his name.

While Western European civilization developed haltingly during the Dark Ages, the art of cryptography was virtually forgotten, although it continued to be practiced in older civilizations such as India and China and in the flourishing Islamic culture. The authority on cryptology, David Kahn, suggests that "as soon as a culture has reached a certain level, probably measured largely by its literacy, cryptography appears spontaneously. . . ."

A few learned and inventive men of the Middle Ages tried their hand at it. The poet Geoffrey Chaucer used six passages of encipherment in his book *The Equatorie of the Planetis*. And in the 13th century, Roger Bacon, a Franciscan friar and scholar, not only studied cryptography but also may have left one of the strangest examples of coded writing in history, the Voynich Manuscript. This mysterious document with its equally mysterious illustrations continues to baffle cryptanalysts today.

Renaissance Cryptography

But if it was not until the Renaissance that cryptography began to be widely studied and practiced. The complex intrigues of the Italian city-states created a need for codes and ciphers and, of course, for experts in the art of cracking them.

Leon Battista Alberti, the illegitimate son of a wealthy Florentine family, was born in 1404 in Genoa and educated at the University of Bologna. He achieved fame as an architect and a painter; he wrote poetry, fables, scientific treatises, books on perspective, color, philosophy, and law; he composed music and was a brilliant organist; he excelled as an athlete. And as if these accomplishments were not enough, Alberti earned for himself the title of Father of Western Cryptology.

One of his contributions to cryptanalysis was to devise the first frequency tables. His 25-page analysis of the frequency and pattern of letters in Latin and Italian is the oldest existing text on cryptanalysis in the West. But Alberti's major contribution was in cryptography. This was a cipher disk that could create many alphabets. Its inventor described it as follows:

"I make two circles out of copper plates. One, the larger, is called stationary, the smaller is called movable. The diameter of the stationary plate is one-ninth greater than that of the movable plate. I divide the circumference of each circle into 24 equal parts. These parts are called cells. In the various cells of the larger circle I write the capital letters, one at a time in red, in the usual order of the letters, A first, B second, C third, and then the rest omitting H and K [and Y] because they are not necessary." In the Latin alphabet, J and U were represented by I and V respectively, and W was omitted. This left 20 letters for the plaintext. Alberti filled the remaining spaces with the first four numerals.

The spaces on the movable disk he filled with a more complete alphabet, not including *j*, *u*, and *w*, but including the word *et* ("and"). This was the cipher alphabet—or rather the arrangement of letters from which alphabets could be made.

"After completing these arrangements," continued Alberti, "we place the smaller circle upon the larger so that a needle driven through the centers of both may serve as axis of both and the movable plate may be revolved around it."

Like most good inventions it was essentially simple. Identical disks were needed by both encipherer and decipherer, who also needed to agree upon an "index letter," which could be any letter chosen from the movable disk. Suppose, for example, that the index letter was *k*. In composing his message, the encipherer would position the *k* next to any capital letter on the

Above: Leon Battista Alberti (1404–72), considered the father of western cryptology. Alberti was also a talented musician, writer, artist, and athlete—a "universal man."

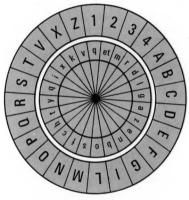

Above: Alberti's cipher disk. To encipher, one aligns the chosen index letter on the inner ring with some letter or number on the outer ring. The plaintext—spelled out on the inner ring—is enciphered by the corresponding letters and digits of the outer ring.

Left: this elaborate cipher disk was designed by Giovanni Battista Porta (born 1535) and uses a set of symbols to encipher the plaintext letters and numbers. Porta contributed to the development of polyalphabetic ciphers and had a genius for solving them.

outer disk, say B. He would then write B at the beginning of his enciphered message to let the decipherer know the correct position of the disk. Once the decipherer had lined up the *k* with the B on his own cipher disk, he could then easily convert each letter of the enciphered message by referring to its plaintext equivalent on the outer disk.

Alberti then complicated the system further. "After writing three or four words, I shall change the position of the index in our formula by turning the circle, so that the index *k* may be, say, under D. So in my message I shall write a capital D and from this point on *k* in the ciphertext will signify no longer B but D, and all the other stationary letters at the top will receive new meanings."

Polyalphabetic Substitution

This innovation, known as *polyalphabetic substitution*, gave cryptography an important new dimension. Within a single message, the same word could appear in totally different guises. For example, the word *arm* could be enciphered DYS, GIC, or

Right: in 1553 Giovanni Belaso suggested the use of a key, called a *countersign*, to indicate which alphabet of the square table had been used. The message consisted of the cipher text with the key written above it. In this example, the receiver would refer to the row beginning with the key letter H on a complete square table, move across that row to the cipher letter B, and follow B up the column to the first row, which gives the letter T.

Right: Girolamo Cardano's idea of using the plaintext as its own key had a major drawback in that it required the recipient to figure out the first word by trial and error before he could use it as the key to encipher the beginning of the second word (*erg*). Once the decipherer got the system going, he could decipher the message with relative ease. The system gave to the decipherer no advantage over an enemy cryptanalyst, and so had very little practical use.

BELASO'S "COUNTERSIGN"

Key:	HASTE	MAKES	WASTE	HASTE	MA
plain	TheDu	keisr	aisin	ganar	my
cipher:	BHYYW	XESYK	WILCR	OAFTX	ZY

CARDANO'S AUTOKEY

key:	SIC	SICE	SICERGOEL
plain:	sic	ergo	elementis
cipher:	NTF	ZCLT	ZVHRYVIPE

NPQ at different settings. Some 50 years later, Trithemius was to improve on Alberti's polyalphabetic substitution by suggesting a change of alphabet with every letter, instead of every few words. But Alberti had already established the principle.

He then embroidered the system by devising a way of enciphering code, using the same cipher disk. He took the four numbers and combined them in two-, three-, and four-digit groups, making a total of 336 codegroups ranging from 11 to 4444. These could be assigned to 336 phrases. The number codegroups could then be enciphered in the same way as one enciphered plaintext letter.

Polyalphabetic substitution was carried a step further by another Italian, Giovanni Battista Belaso. This otherwise obscure man is remembered for a booklet, published in 1553, in which he suggested the use of a key, or *countersign*, that could be used to govern the choice of the alphabet in which a given letter of plaintext was to be enciphered. "This countersign," wrote Belaso, "may consist of some words in Italian or Latin, or any other language, and the words may be as few or as many as desired. Then we take the words we wish to write, and put them on paper, writing them not too close together. Then over each of the letters we place a letter of our countersign." The countersign letter above each letter of the enciphered message indicates which alphabet has been used to encipher that particular letter (see top diagram on this page).

THE CARDANO GRILL

HOPING TO FIND YOU AN EMPIRE STYLE
5   6 3

ARMOIRE OF SIZE YOU SPECIFIED. I
12   13

THINK EDWARD MIGHT KNOW A GOOD
2   11   10   4

DEALER IN MONTPELLIER. ARE YOU
8

INTERESTED IN BRASS CANDELABRA? I
9

SAW A PAIR YESTERDAY IN VERY GOOD
1   7

CONDITION FOR 300 FRANCS - 18th C.

Above: Girolamo Cardano, the frontispiece from his book *De Rerum Varietate*, in which he discussed a miscellany of subjects, including cryptology.

Left: a stylized version of Cardano's grille. In reality the grille is a sheet of stiff material that is placed over the innocuous-looking message that has been constructed around the real message. The real message can easily be read by following the order of the numbered windows.

Girolamo Cardano, a Milanese physician, mathematician, and writer of books on a multitude of subjects, also turned his hand to cryptology. He used the plaintext as its own key (see the lower diagram opposite), which avoided the problem of communicating the key separately to the decipherer. Unfortunately, the legitimate decipherer was in the same position as the enemy cryptanalyst; he had to figure out the first word before he could get the key started, as it were. The possibility of deciphering the first cipher group incorrectly and so getting the key—and consequently the message—wrong placed Cardano's idea in the category of unrealized inspirations.

He is remembered more for a steganographic device called the *Cardano grille*. This is a piece of stiff cardboard or other material perforated with several rectangular holes, the same height as ordinary script, at irregular intervals. Some of the holes are wide enough for a whole word, others for just a letter or a syllable. They are numbered in random order. The card is then placed on a sheet of paper and the message spelled out in the order dictated by the numbers. When the card is removed the message appears a jumble of letters. It is then further disguised by incorporating it into an innocent-looking message, as shown in the diagram on page 21. The decoder, who has an identical grille, merely places it on top of the letter and reads the message in the correct order.

One drawback to this technique is that the covering message

Above: Blaise de Vigenère, a 16th-century French diplomat and scholar, wrote a 600-page work on cryptology entitled *Traicté des Chiffres* and also invented a workable autokey.

Right: Vigenère's ingenious system, like Cardano's, used the plaintext as a key to encipher itself. The main improvement was that the recipient of the message had the first key letter (D), which told him which alphabet in the table had been used to encipher the first plaintext letter. He could then convert the cipher text X into its plaintext equivalent *a*. The A identified the alphabet according to which the I was enciphered, and so on.

may be awkwardly phrased and thus arouse suspicions on the part of anyone intercepting it that it may contain a secret message. Nevertheless, it was widely used by European governments in the 16th and 17th centuries.

For the benefit of cryptanalysts, Cardano devised a technique of surreptitiously reading correspondence. One inserted a thin rod into the envelope, wound the letter onto the rod, and removed it. After its contents were noted, the letter was replaced.

It was during this period that reading other governments' correspondence began to be a full-time job. Nations now maintained permanent ambassadors in various foreign courts, and these ambassadors sent frequent communications home. By the end of the 16th century most governments had at least one cipher secretary to encipher and decipher messages, and sometimes a cryptanalytic specialist as well.

The powerful Venetian Republic had perhaps the most efficient "black chamber" of the day, thanks largely to its cipher secretary and skilled cryptanalyst, Giovanni Soro. He and his two assistants worked in a room in the Doge's Palace, behind barred doors. When a message was intercepted it was taken immediately to this chamber, and the secretaries were required to stay there until they deciphered it. Their employers, the Council of Ten, rewarded initiative in code-making and code-breaking. A secretary who made a valuable suggestion was given a raise, and contests were occasionally held to encourage the devising of new ciphers. However, a secretary who revealed any of his government's cryptologic secrets to outsiders was punished by death.

While the Italians were taking the lead in cryptology, other nations were also producing experts on the subject. One of these was the Frenchman Blaise de Vigenère. After an active career as a diplomat, during which he became acquainted with Italian cryptologists, Vigenère retired to write books. In his *Traicté des Chiffres*, published in 1586, he included a number of ciphers, polyalphabets, key words, phrases, and numbers, and also described his autokey system.

Like Cardano's autokey, it was based on its own plaintext but it had the advantage of using a prearranged key letter or

VIGENERE'S AUTOKEY

Key:	D A	U N O	M D	E L E T E R N E
plain:	a u	n o m	d e	L'eternel
cipher:	X I	A H G	U P	T M L S H I X T

priming key, known to both encipherer and decipherer. This priming key indicated the alphabet that had been used to encipher the first letter. With this information, the decipherer could substitute the plaintext letter, which was also the second letter of the autokey. By repeating the process for each consecutive letter, he could spell out the plaintext message (see the diagram on the facing page).

English Plots and Codes

The latter part of the 16th century was an especially turbulent age for England, largely as a result of Henry VIII's break with the Roman Catholic Church. After his death in 1547, the succession to the English throne was a hot issue both within the country and on the continent. Naturally, the Pope and the Catholic powers wanted to bring England back into the fold, and when Henry's Protestant daughter Elizabeth ascended the throne, all sorts of schemes were hatched to marry Elizabeth to a Catholic prince, or to dethrone her and install a Catholic in her place.

Elizabeth was well aware that her situation was a precarious one. Fortunately, she had an efficient and large—for those days—

Above: Sir Francis Walsingham, a minister and diplomat under Queen Elizabeth I. Vigilant in his efforts to protect the queen from her enemies, he created a very effective intelligence network.

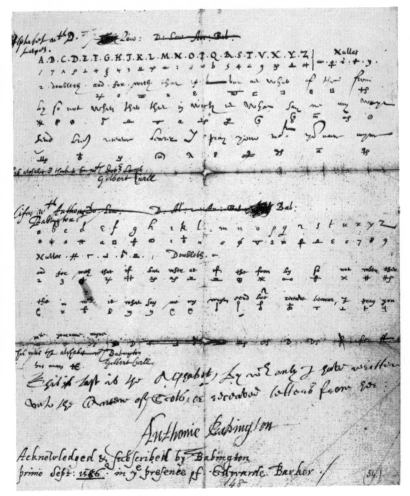

Left: a page of codes used by the advisers and secretaries of Mary Queen of Scots. The signature of her secretary Gilbert Curll, who usually did the enciphering of Mary's letters, and that of Anthony Babington, the chief conspirator in the plot against Queen Elizabeth, are included toward the bottom of the page of codes.

intelligence service. More than 50 spies worked for the queen throughout Europe under the able direction of Sir Francis Walsingham. It was Walsingham who astutely procured the services of Thomas Phelippes, England's first great cryptanalyst.

While still quite young, Phelippes was employed by Walsingham as one of his confidential assistants. He had traveled widely in France, and in 1577 Walsingham—who had previously relied on the services of the skilled Flemish cryptanalyst Philip van Marnix—dispatched the young Englishman to Paris to decipher any intercepted messages that came his way. Phelippes did not disappoint his employer. He was able to solve not only those ciphers originally written in French, but also those originally written in Latin and Italian. Later, back in England, he was to help Walsingham bring about the downfall of Mary Queen of Scots.

Mary Stuart was Queen Elizabeth's cousin and next in the line of succession to the English throne, as Elizabeth had no children. In the eyes of Catholic Europe, Elizabeth was illegitimate and Mary was the rightful queen. Driven from Scotland in 1568 by a rebellion on the part of some Scottish nobles, Mary sought refuge in England. But the various schemes concocted by her supporters to make her Queen of England brought Mary under suspicion. There was no proof of her complicity in these plots, but Elizabeth thought it prudent to keep her cousin under house arrest. Mary was living in the castle of Chartley when, in 1586, Walsingham saw an opportunity to obtain conclusive evidence against her and so eliminate this threat to his queen.

He obtained the services of Gilbert Gifford, a young Catholic who was in trouble with the authorities and willing to help Walsingham in order to save his own neck. Gifford soon ingratiated himself with one of Mary's devoted courtiers, Anthony Babington. He also went to Chartley and gained the trust of Mary herself, to whom he professed his willingness to die, if need be, for her sake. Babington and Mary swallowed the bait, and Gifford became her messenger. He soon discovered a way of getting her letters past the guards by hiding them in a beer barrel.

The method was so successful that the French ambassador in London entrusted Gifford with all the correspondence he had been holding for Mary. These letters had been accumulating over the past two years, because previous efforts to get them through to the captive queen had failed. Before smuggling them into Chartley, Gifford handed them to Walsingham, who had them copied and passed those in cipher on to Phelippes. Then the letters were carefully resealed with forged seals and conveyed to Mary.

This correspondence and subsequent letters between Babington and his friends, dutifully handed to Walsingham by Gifford, revealed a well-organized plot to assassinate Elizabeth and Walsingham and—with military help from Philip II of Spain—

Right: a 17th-century woodcut gloats over the failure of the plot to place the Catholic Mary Queen of Scots on the English throne. On the left Babington is shown laying his plans. On the right he and the other plotters are executed.

Below right: the execution of Mary Queen of Scots at Fotheringay Castle on February 8, 1587. Although she had been found guilty of treason three months earlier, the order for her death was not signed by Queen Elizabeth until February—and then only with great reluctance.

Below: a portrait of the young Queen of Scots by a French artist. Mary spent her youth in France; her first husband was the heir to its throne.

In quo quis peccat
In eo punitur.

Hi mihi sunt Comites quos ipsa pericula ducunt

R.H.

Babington with his Complices in St Giles fields

to install Mary as Queen of England. The assassination of Elizabeth was to be carried out by six English courtiers, whose code-names, however, even Phelippes was unable to translate.

For a while, Walsingham did nothing. He simply waited for the moment when Mary would have to commit herself in writing. Finally, he obtained a letter from Babington to Mary describing the plot to her. Walsingham sent the letter on its way and waited for Mary's reply. After an agonizingly long week, the reply came. It acknowledged "the enterprise" and advised Babington of ways "to bring it to good success."

Neither of the letters included the names of the conspirators. So Walsingham tried an audacious ploy. He had someone—probably Phelippes—forge a postscript, in the correct cipher, to Mary's letter. It asked Babington for "the names and qualities of the six gentlemen which are to accomplish the designment."

As it turned out, however, the postscript was unnecessary. In an attempt to get a passport for a trip to the Continent, Babington had to come to Walsingham. While dining with one of Walsingham's men, he caught a glimpse of a warrant for his own arrest. Predictably, Babington made an escape, and the hue and cry that followed alerted the other six conspirators, who also tried to flee the country. A watch was set up at all the ports, and within a month all six, as well as Babington, were captured. Shortly after their execution, Mary herself was brought to trial and convicted on the evidence of her enciphered letters. On February 8, 1587 she was beheaded.

Nearly 60 years later, Mary's grandson, King Charles I of England, also had his mail read by an English cryptanalyst. This was John Wallis, a noted mathematician and clergyman who got into code-breaking more or less accidentally and established a reputation by solving a cryptogram that had defied decipherment for more than two years. It took Wallis three months to solve it, but his feat so impressed Members of Parliament that they enlisted his help in their struggle with the king. During the Civil War Wallis solved a number of dispatches from the king that the Parliamentarians managed to intercept. Eventually, in 1649, Charles I was beheaded; and for the next 11 years the Puritan party ruled England.

Wallis's code-breaking ability was so highly respected that when Charles II returned to England as monarch in 1660, he sought out Wallis and employed him—despite the fact that Wallis had worked for his father's enemies. Eventually Wallis became chaplain to the king. According to the 17th-century writer John Aubrey, Wallis was "a person of reall worth" who "may stand very gloriously upon his owne basis, and need not be beholding to any man for Fame, yet he is so extremely greedy of glorie, that he steales feathers from others to adorn his own cap; e.g., he lies at watch at Sir Christopher Wren's discourses, Mr. Robert Hooke's, Dr. William Holder, &c; putts downe their notions in his Note booke, and then prints it, without owneing the author. This frequently, of which they complain."

Wallis knew his value to the government as a cryptanalyst, and frequently raised his fees. He also got the government to pay for his grandson's tutoring in cryptanalysis—although he himself once implicitly admitted that the subject could not be taught: "every new Cipher allmost being contrived in a new Way, which doth not admit any constant Method for the finding of it out."

Evidently his grandson, William Blencowe, had a talent for the work, for on Wallis's death in 1703, the 20-year-old Blencowe assumed his post. Blencowe, in fact, was the first English cryptanalyst to bear the title Decypherer and to receive a regular salary for his services. He did not hold the job for long, however, for he committed suicide in 1712. He was succeeded briefly by a rather inept practitioner of the art, who was himself succeeded by Edward Willes, whose family were to retain the post for three generations.

Willes managed not only to combine cryptanalysis with his career as a clergyman but also to rise to more exalted posts within the Church as a result of his code-breaking services to the Crown. By the time his eldest son was appointed Decypherer in 1742, Willes had been made Bishop of Bath and Wells.

Perhaps the highlight of his cryptanalytic career was when he testified in the House of Lords against a fellow clergyman, Francis Atterbury, Bishop of Rochester. Atterbury was accused of trying to set a pretender on the throne in place of King George I. The evidence produced by Willes and another decypherer consisted of intercepted correspondence between Atterbury and his co-conspirators. Realizing how damning the evidence against him was, Atterbury kept questioning Willes, hoping to throw doubt on his ability to decipher the letters. Willes, not wishing to impart too many of his secrets, refused to be drawn. Eventually, with the wildly protesting Atterbury and his counsel sent out of the chamber, the Lords voted "that it is not consistent with the public Safety to ask the Decypherers any Questions, which may tend to discover the Art or Mystery of Decyphering." Atterbury was convicted and banished from Britain.

Willes and his descendants were joined by other cryptanalysts and were known collectively as the Decyphering Branch. They had no official quarters and worked mainly in their homes, receiving work by special messengers from the Secret Office and the Private Office. These bureaus were responsible for the opening of foreign and domestic mail respectively. The act of 1657 that established the postal service declared frankly that the mails were a good way to detect subversive activity, and subsequent laws confirmed the right of the government to open private correspondence. The staff of these two offices worked in secrecy, opening letters and parcels and resealing them so deftly that no one could tell they had been opened. Those in cipher were sent to members of the Decyphering Branch. The very existence of this bureau was known to only a handful of people,

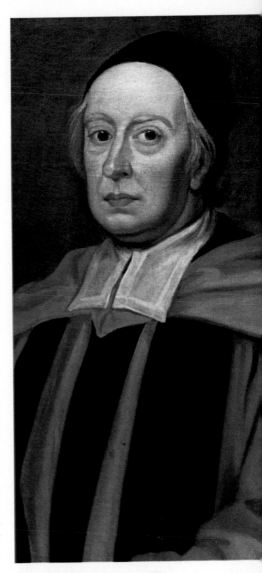

John Wallis (1616–1703) was not only a clergyman and a brilliant mathematician but also England's first great cryptanalyst. He served under the Parliamentary government and under Charles II and William and Mary. His solution of the correspondence between the French King Louis XIV and his ambassador in Poland in 1689 helped to thwart Louis's designs in that nation.

Above: Edward Willes (1694–1773), another English clergyman-decipherer. Perhaps his most dramatic achievement was deciphering correspondence of Francis Atterbury, Bishop of Rochester, that revealed his involvement in a conspiracy to restore the Stuarts to the throne.

Above right: King James II of England being shown his infant son by the Papal Nuncio. The child, born in 1688, only a few months before his father was forced to flee, became, after James's death, the Pretender to the throne, supported by Bishop Atterbury.

but its work—which included solutions of messages from all over Europe, and later from the United States—repeatedly proved of value to the government.

French Cryptanalysis

During the 17th century the French government was fortunate in having the services of the skilled cryptanalyst Antoine Rossignol. The son of a prominent family of the city of Albi in southern France, Rossignol began his career in 1628, when the nearby town of Réalmont was under siege. Réalmont, a Protestant stronghold, was surrounded by government troops led by the Prince de Condé. For several days the inhabitants continued to fire on Condé's army, while the prince waited impatiently for a sign of weakness.

Then, on the fifth day of the siege, a citizen of Réalmont slipped outside the walls and set off to get reinforcements. He was captured by Condé's men, who quickly appropriated the letter he was carrying. It was written in cipher, and no one on Condé's staff could read it. So the prince sent it to young Rossignol in Albi.

Rossignol deciphered the message on the spot and told the prince that the inhabitants of Réalmont were desperately in need of ammunition. The prince sent the cryptogram back to Réalmont. A week later, the town capitulated.

Soon after this incident, another Protestant town, the port of La Rochelle, also fell victim to Rossignol's cryptanalytic skill. Some enciphered letters were intercepted and passed to the Catholic commander, Cardinal Richelieu. The cardinal passed them on to Rossignol, who read them easily and reported that the citizens were awaiting help from the English. Armed with this information, Richelieu's forces prevented the English ships from landing. Within a month, La Rochelle surrendered.

Rossignol's ability soon brought him into favor with King Louis XIII and later with Louis XIV. In the Sun King's splendid Palace of Versailles, Rossignol worked in a room next to the king's study. The financial rewards he received for his services enabled him to live in great style. He built a small chateau near Paris, with gardens designed by Le Nôtre, the landscape gardener of Versailles. He was universally praised: the Duke of Saint-Simon called him "the most skillful decipherer of Europe"; he was given a two-page entry, complete with portrait, in Charles Perrault's *Illustrious Men Who Have Appeared During This Century*; the poet Boisrobert, his friend, wrote a poem in his honor, including such lines as the following: "There's not a thing beneath the skies That can be hidden from thine eyes. . . ."

Rossignol also made a significant contribution to cryptography. For more than 400 years, European cryptography was dominated by the type of code called the *nomenclator*. This was something of a cross between a code and a cipher, containing a mixture of word equivalents and letter substitutions. Nomenclators were relatively easy to solve because both the plaintext elements and the code or cipher elements were listed in ascending order—alphabetical or numerical.

Rossignol pointed out that part of his success in solving cryptograms was due to their simplicity. If, for instance, the cryptanalyst discovered that 213 meant *send* and 270 meant *stop*, he knew that 256 could not represent *return*, as this would necessarily be represented by some number lower than 213. He would also know that the code number for *signal* must come between 213 and 270. Rossignol introduced the idea of assigning the code elements at random, so that 213 might stand for *send* and 182 for *stop* and 589 for *return*. The encipherer would have a list arranged according to the code elements, in their alphabetical or numerical order, so that he could easily find their plaintext equivalents.

Throughout the 17th and 18th centuries, black chambers sprang up throughout Europe. Probably the most efficient of them operated in Vienna, capital city of the sprawling Holy Roman Empire. It was called the Geheime Kabinets-Kanzlei (roughly "Secret Government Office").

By 7:00 a.m., the morning mail for the foreign embassies in Vienna had been delivered to the secret office. There, the letters were opened and read and the important and enciphered

Above: the great French crypt-analyst Antoine Rossignol (1600–82). He established his usefulness to the state by deciphering the correspondence of the Huguenots during the religious wars of the day.

Below: the siege of La Rochelle, a Huguenot stronghold that was taken by Richlieu.

passages copied out quickly and accurately. The letters were then replaced in their envelopes and resealed and were on their way to their legitimate destinations within two and a half hours of their interception.

Half an hour later, at 10:00 a.m., letters passing through Vienna en route to other cities were brought to the office for scrutiny. These were back in the mail by 2:00 p.m. A third delivery, the interceptions from the police force, arrived at 11:00 a.m. At 4:00 p.m., the last of the day's mail—the outgoing letters from the embassies—arrived and were copied swiftly so that they too could continue on their journey that same evening.

The staff of the Geheime Kabinets-Kanzlei had to be adept at several tasks. They needed not only an adroit cryptanalytic brain but also deft fingers, able to melt off a seal and replace it with a counterfeit that would fool the recipient. They had to have a flair for languages. If a letter was in a language unknown to any of the staff, someone set about learning that language. Astonishingly, this well-oiled machine was operated by teams of not more than 10 men, who handled between 80 and 100 letters each day. Because of the strain of the work, the men worked alternate weeks. Their basic salary was not particularly high, but for every solution achieved they received a substantial bonus, personally presented by the emperor. The Empress Maria Theresa took great interest in the work of her black

Below: a triple portrait of Cardinal Richelieu (1585–1642), chief minister under Louis XIII. In the course of his war against the Huguenots, he employed Rossignol, whose cryptanalytic skill helped him take La Rochelle (opposite).

chamber and often conferred with them about the ciphers used by her ambassadors. In a single month, March 1751, she distributed 3730 florins in bonuses.

The ability of the Viennese black chamber was well-known outside Austria. Its director wrote in 1751: "This is the 18th cipher that we have got through during the course of the year . . . we are regarded, unhappily, as being too able in this art, and this thought makes the courts that fear that we can engross their correspondence change their keys at every instant, so to speak, each time sending ones more difficult and more laborious to decipher."

Heads of state have not always been so well served by their cryptanalysts or cryptographers. Napoleon used a *petit chiffre*, or "little cipher," composed of a mere 200 signs, throughout most of his campaigns. His generals, who were not particularly adept at this aspect of strategy, tended to be careless about it. As a rule they only partly enciphered their messages, and on more than one occasion a general got the cipher totally muddled. At the Battle of Leipzig, in 1813, one general's inability to encipher a message correctly resulted in Napoleon's orders being disobeyed—a contributing factor in his defeat. During the disastrous Russian campaign of the previous winter, the weakness of the *petit chiffre* had provided the Russians with another advantage. Their cryptanalysts easily solved it and were then able to read the French army's messages.

Somewhat ironically, in view of Napoleon's cryptologic weakness, one of the best-known of all ciphers bears the name of the military academy he founded, St Cyr. The *St Cyr cipher*, or *slide* (see diagram opposite), is a card on which is printed the alphabet, plus a movable strip on which the alphabet is printed twice, which is threaded through two slits in the card. To encipher a message, one moves the slide until the key letter is placed under the A in the stationary, or plaintext, alphabet. The other plaintext letters can then be enciphered with the equivalents immediately below them.

Obviously the simplicity of the system was a great advantage. Messages could be enciphered quickly without the risk of choosing the wrong letter—as might often happen in searching through a table of multiple alphabets—and deciphering was equally easy, provided one had the key letter.

The Playfair Cipher

Another famous cipher of the 19th century was a British invention. This was the Playfair cipher. It was really invented by Sir Charles Wheatstone, a scientist with wide-ranging talents and interests who had, among his other achievements, devised an electric telegraph before Morse did. Wheatstone's cipher was enthusiastically taken up by his friend and fellow scientist Baron Playfair, who demonstrated it at a dinner in 1854 attended by Prince Albert and the future Prime Minister

Above: Napoleon at the Battle of Leipzig, which he lost in October 1813. Although a superb strategist, Napoleon placed little importance on cryptography, and his generals tended to be careless about enciphering their messages. A bungled encipherment contributed to the Leipzig defeat.

Right: the St. Cyr cipher, or slide, named after the military academy founded by Napoleon. The movable strip can produce many cipher alphabets.

ABCDEFGHIJKLMNOPQRSTUVWXYZ

| ABCDEFGHIJK | QRSTUVWXYZABCDEFGHIJKLMNOP | VWXYZ |

Below: the Playfair cipher, a square formed by a key word filled out with the remaining alphabet letters not used in it (top). Encipherment is in paired letters. Plaintext letter pairs in the same row or column become the letter to their right or below—PL to AM and MO to OF, for example. Pairs elsewhere are replaced by the letter at the junction of the row and column each of the pair is in. In TH, then, T becomes R (center) and H becomes K (bottom).

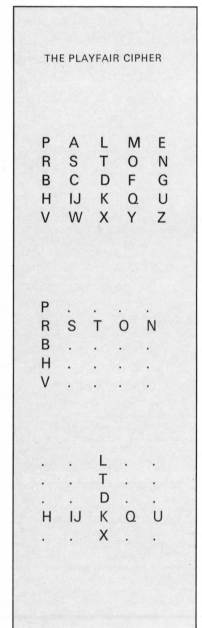

THE PLAYFAIR CIPHER

P	A	L	M	E
R	S	T	O	N
B	C	D	F	G
H	IJ	K	Q	U
V	W	X	Y	Z

Lord Palmerston. Playfair never claimed the invention as his own, but his championing of it resulted in his own name being attached to it.

In essence, the cipher in its simplified form is a block of letters, with the key word occupying the top line, and perhaps part or all of the next line also, as shown (left). The word must be one containing no repeated letters. The rest of the square is filled with the remaining letters of the alphabet, with I and J considered as one letter. To encipher, one first breaks up the plaintext into pairs of letters, or digraphs. Double letters must be split with an x, so that they would not be recognizable as the same letter when enciphered. Thus, the word *battalion* would be rendered BA TX TA LI ON. These digraphs are enciphered in one of three ways: (1) If both letters are in the same row, they are each enciphered with the letter to the right (the letter at the extreme right being enciphered with the letter at the beginning of the row). (2) If they are both in the same column, they are enciphered with the letter immediately below (the bottom letter by the one at the top of the column). (3) If they are in neither the same row nor the same column, each is enciphered with the letter in its own row that is in the same column as its pair letter.

The Playfair has several advantages. For one thing, the use of digraphs concealed the frequency of plaintext letters. The common letter *e*, for example, would be enciphered P (as on the left) if its pair letter is in the same row, N if the pair is in the same column, and either P, A, L, or M if the pair is somewhere

Above left: Sir Charles
Wheatstone, the physicist who
invented the Playfair cipher—
named for his friend Baron
Playfair, who popularized it.

Above: Wheatstone's crypto-
graph. The outer circle contains
the letters of the alphabet.
For encipherment, the two gear-
connected hands are first
aligned. The long hand is then
used to spell out the plaintext, while the shorter of the
hands automatically selects
the cipher text equivalents
from the inner circle. Its
letters can be changed according to the key word, the letters
of which are followed by
the remaining letters of the
alphabet in a known pattern.

else in the square. This puts the cryptanalyst at a great disadvantage, for he cannot use frequency tables in cracking the
cipher. From the point of view of the encipherer, the Playfair
has the advantage of being relatively simple to use. It served as
the British field cipher for many years.

In the 19th century, the political reforms that curtailed the
power of monarchs and their ministers in many countries also
closed down the black chambers. In 1844, the British government ceased the interception of diplomatic correspondence.
Four years later, the Austrian Geheime Kabinets-Kanzlei was
abolished. In that same politically turbulent year of 1848, the
French Cabinet Noir, which had been rather inactive since
the revolution of 1789, also folded.

The United States, which from the beginning had declared
its abhorrence of tyrannical governments and their machinery,
lacked any sort of black chamber. Of course, the making and
breaking of codes necessarily played a part in America's wars.
And the author of the Declaration of Independence, the
versatile Thomas Jefferson, devised an ingenious little gadget,
called a *wheel cipher*, that is still used today by the U.S. Navy.
But it was not until this century, when the United States had
become a world power, that cryptanalysis became part of the
machinery of its government. This was largely due to the efforts
of Herbert Osborne Yardley.

Herbert Osborne Yardley

Yardley had intended to become a criminal lawyer, but while
still in his early 20s he got sidetracked into working as a code
clerk in the State Department. The codes fascinated him, and
one evening he had a try at cracking the code used by President
Wilson in communicating with his closest advisors. Yardley
solved it in a few hours.

When the United States entered World War I, Yardley
managed to sell the War Office the idea of setting up a code-
breaking department. At the age of 27 he became the head of
this new department of the Military Intelligence Division—
MI8.

MI8 grew rapidly. Perhaps its most notable achievement
during the war was the solving of a 424-letter cryptogram found
among the possessions of a German named Lothar Witzke,
who was being held on suspicion of being responsible for an
explosion. The cryptogram, found when Witzke was captured
in Mexico, was passed around MI8 until it reached Dr John
M. Manly, a philologist and expert on Chaucer. Manly and his
associate Edith Rickert worked for three days before they
unraveled the complexities of its 12-step transposition and
obtained the following message:

"The bearer of this is a subject of the [German] Empire who
travels as a Russian under the name of Pablo Waberski. He is a
German secret agent. Please furnish him on request protection

and assistance; also advance him on demand up to 1000 pesos of Mexican gold and send his code telegrams to this embassy as official consular dispatches." The letter was signed by Heinrich von Eckhardt, the German minister in Mexico City, who was also involved, indirectly, in the embarrassing incident of the Zimmermann telegram.

This message was more than enough to convict the young German, and he was sentenced to death. He was later reprieved by President Wilson and released from prison in 1923.

Meanwhile, Yardley traveled to Europe in search of any methods of code-breaking he could elicit from friendly nations. He was allowed only a few glimpses of British techniques. In France he spent considerable time with the greatest French expert, Georges Painvin, but was never able to penetrate to the heart of the French intelligence service.

When the war was over he returned to the States, where his persuasive manner was more successful. He succeeded in getting the Secretary of State and the Chief of Staff to agree to his setting up a permanent department for code and cipher investigation.

On October 1, 1919 the American black chamber—which actually became known by that evocative name—began its existence in New York City. Part of its funds came—secretly—from the State Department, which meant that it could not function within Washington, D.C. It had several temporary homes before settling into Number 141 East 37th Street. It operated in the strictest secrecy. Yardley and his 20 colleagues maintained constant vigilance over the security of the office. Mail was sent to a cover address; locks were often changed. Even so, the office was eventually broken into, and the black chamber moved again to other Manhattan premises.

Most of its early work consisted in trying to break the Japanese codes. The Japanese language itself was a problem. In their telegrams, the Japanese replaced the characters of their language with words spelled out in Latin letters. But even after the cryptanalysts deciphered the message, they still needed an English translation of the spelled-out Japanese. For a while, Yardley was aided—if unwittingly—by a missionary who had spent some time in Japan and who translated telegrams into English until, after several months, it dawned on him that he was assisting in espionage against a nation with whom, at that time, the United States was at peace. On his resignation, a black chamber employee who had managed to learn Japanese took up the task.

Through the work of the black chamber, the U.S. government learned that the Japanese delegation to the world conference limiting naval tonnage would, if pushed, accept a 10:6 ratio instead of their original demand for a 10:7 tonnage ratio between the United States and Britain and their own nation. After this glimpse of their opponent's hand, the United States and Britain simply applied the requisite pressure.

Other nations, too, were subjected to the scrutiny of the black chamber. It cracked the codes of Argentina, Brazil, Chile, China, Costa Rica, Cuba, Britain, France, Germany, Japan, Liberia, Mexico, Nicaragua, Panama, Peru, San Salvador, Santo Domingo (later the Dominican Republic), the Soviet Union, and Spain.

In 1929, with the inauguration of the Hoover Administration, the black chamber fell out of favor. Secretary of State Henry L. Stimson was shocked to learn of its existence. "Gentlemen do not read each other's mail," he said. All State Department funds to the chamber were cut off, and within a few months it closed its doors.

Like many other Americans, Yardley soon found himself caught in the ruthless economics of the Depression. Fortunately, however, he had something to sell: the inside story of the black chamber. His book *The American Black Chamber* was serialized in the *Saturday Evening Post* and published in 1931. It was an immediate success. Official disclaimers from the government failed to diminish sales, and the book was soon translated into several foreign languages. In Japan it sold 33,119 copies—more, per capita, than in the United States. The Japanese government received it with cries of outrage against the United States and mutual recriminations among themselves. Reaction in the Japanese press was mixed. One English-language paper, the *Japan Chronicle*, echoed Secretary Stimson's feelings, declaring: "It is so much like steaming open people's letters—a thing which is distinctly not done." But the *Japan Times* took a more realistic view of the matter, that more nearly reflected the history of nations' dealings with each other: "Trying to decipher the other nation's code," it said, "is part of the game."

The American cryptanalyst H. O. Yardley and an associate, J. Rives Childs, on duty at the Hotel Crillon, Paris, during the Peace Conference in 1919. In the same year Yardley established in New York City the first American secret "black chamber."

Cryptanalysis in World War I

3

Relatively few people in the British Admiralty knew what was going on in Room 40. It was but one of dozens of offices in which civil servants dealt with the paper work generated by one of the bloodiest conflicts in human history: World War I. But the papers handled in Room 40 were of a rather special nature; they were secret messages sent by the enemy, and it was the task of the people in Room 40 to decipher them.

The bureau had come into being early in the war in an almost casual way, when the director of naval intelligence sought the help of an amateur cryptanalyst, Sir Alfred Ewing, in solving some intercepted German coded radio messages. Ewing spent the next few weeks boning up on codes and ciphers of all kinds and enlisting the help of others like himself who had a gift for solving puzzles. Probably none of this little group of novice cryptanalysts guessed at the time that by the end of the war their office would have become the most efficient code-breaking establishment in the world.

Cryptanalysis played a crucial role in World War I. The invention of telegraphy and radio had made possible rapid communication, but the ease with which these communications could be intercepted by the enemy—as contrasted with the difficulty of intercepting a message sent by hand—meant that it was essential to put radio and telegraph messages into extremely complex codes and ciphers. The increasingly sophisticated cryptography stimulated the development of cryptanalysis on a large and intensive scale.

Room 40 had its counterparts in other countries, including Germany. And when the United States finally entered the war in 1917, it set up its own cryptanalytic department, then called MI8. But it was the British and the French who achieved the most dramatic and decisive code-breaking successes of World War I.

One of these was the deciphering of the Germans' formidable ADFGX cipher by the French, which thwarted the last big German offensive. The other was the British solving of the Zimmermann telegram, which succeeded in bringing the United States into the war at a time when the Allies were on the verge of exhaustion.

Above: the combined Houses of Congress greeting with enthusiasm President Wilson's call for a declaration of war on April 2, 1917. One event that forced the President's hand was the decoding of the Zimmermann telegram, in which Germany offered Mexico a large chunk of U.S. territory. Right: the Zimmermann telegram as it was sent from Washington to Mexico City. The original had been sent to the German ambassador in Washington in Code 0075, and it was this version that the British code-breakers had intercepted and largely completed decoding. The German ambassador had the message re-encoded and sent off in Code 13040 because the minister in Mexico City did not have Code 0075. A British agent in Mexico City managed to obtain this version, which then enabled the London code-breakers to fill the gaps in the original.

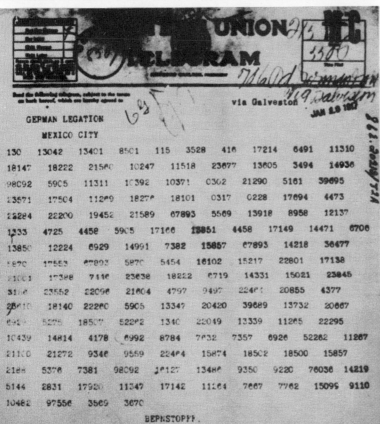

Above: Arthur Zimmermann,
German Foreign Minister in 1917
His audacious plan to secure
the cooperation of Mexico in
the event of war with the United States was thwarted by
the code-breakers of Room 40.

The Zimmermann Telegram

In January 1917 the war had become a seemingly endless and futile struggle, with both sides sacrificing men by the thousands and gaining almost nothing. In a single day during the Battle of the Somme, the British had lost 60,000 men; half a million on each side had died at Verdun.

The one ray of hope for the Allies was that the United States would enter the war. For three years the Americans had refused to join the Allies. The strong isolationist element in the States was personified by President Wilson, who had steadily resisted all efforts on the part of the Allies and their supporters in America to draw the country into the conflict, and who clung to the belief that he could arrange a "peace without victory" between the combatants. For the Germans, of course, it was crucial to keep the Americans out of the war. Yet their one hope of defeating the Allies was to begin unrestricted submarine warfare, which would mean torpedoing ships—including American ships—that were bringing supplies to Britain and other Western powers. Such attacks would almost certainly bring a declaration of war from the United States.

The German Foreign Minister Arthur Zimmermann then conceived a plan that, in the event of such a declaration, might divert the United States from the war in Europe and keep her busy elsewhere. In order to carry out his plan Zimmermann had to contact the German ambassador in Washington. He had several ways of doing this.

One of Britain's first acts when the war started in 1914 was to cut Germany's transatlantic cables. Lacking a direct telegraphic link with the United States, Germany had obtained permission from the officially neutral, but pro-German, Swedes to use Sweden's Stockholm-London-Washington link. When the British protested, Sweden promised to desist but then offered the Germans an alternative route. This route went from Stockholm all the way down to Buenos Aires. From that point, messages could be sent over German lines up through South America to Mexico City, and then to Washington.

Besides the 7000-mile "Swedish Roundabout," the Germans had another link with Washington: the American diplomatic cables. Late in 1916 the German ambassador in Washington had persuaded Wilson that efforts to arrange peace would be greatly facilitated if his government in Berlin could communicate directly with Washington. The agreement included permission for the Germans to use their own code—a contravention of the normal international practice of requiring a belligerent's message to be submitted in clear text for transmission in the neutral country's own code. Both Wilson and his confidant Colonel Edward M. House were under the impression that the German government was sincerely dedicated to a fair peace settlement. They never imagined that Germany would repay this naive trust by using the cable to convey a message aimed against America herself.

In order to make sure his message arrived, Zimmermann decided to use both the American cable and the Swedish Roundabout. What he did not know was that both routes touched England, and that the British were regularly decoding German messages sent via these routes. The British had not protested when Sweden violated her promise not to relay German messages; more could be gained, they decided, by seeing what the Germans had to say. Similarly, they made no protest at the American deal with Germany, but quietly continued their equally illegal eavesdropping on the State Department cable, in the hope of discovering something valuable.

By the time Zimmermann sent his telegram, Room 40 was greatly expanded and had moved to larger quarters, though it continued to operate under the original name. Its chief was Captain William Reginald Hall, of the Royal Navy. Hall was an extraordinary man, supremely confident and a brilliant strategist, who had a powerful effect on everyone who knew him. "When . . . he spoke to you," wrote Francis Toye, one of the cryptanalysts of Room 40, "you felt that you would do anything, anything at all, to merit his approval." His remarkable penetrating eyes missed nothing. "Hall can look through you," said American ambassador Page, "and see the very muscular movements of your immortal soul. . . ."

Hall was fortunate in having a staff of skilled and dedicated people, many of whom had made names for themselves—or would later make names for themselves—in various professions. A young wounded officer named Edward Molyneux, who sorted incoming messages, later became a famous fashion designer. Francis Toye became a well-known music critic. Another cryptanalyst, Ronald Knox, later became a Roman Catholic priest and made a new translation of the Bible. A sprinkling of academics from Oxford, Cambridge, and other universities applied their intellects to the flood of cryptic messages that poured into Room 40.

One of these scholars was Reverend William Montgomery, an expert on early Church history, an expert translator of German, and one of Room 40's most brilliant cryptanalysts. He and a younger colleague, Nigel de Grey, had been working on Code 0075, one of several diplomatic codes used by the Germans. Room 40 had already obtained several telegrams in this code, addressed to various German missions around the world, and Montgomery and de Grey had made some progress in breaking it.

Codes, in one sense, are less mysterious than ciphers. A code exchanges one complete word for another—or, more commonly, uses a nonsense group of letters or numerals in place of the word. Thus, the word *apple* might, in code, be 75976 or TROJU. Five-letter or five-numeral groups are often preferred to shorter groups, because they allow a larger vocabulary for the code than a three- or four-item group would. Moreover, the use of five items reduces the risk of error in sending a message in

Above: Rear-Admiral Sir Reginald Hall who, as Captain Hall, directed the activities of Room 40. He had a genius for getting the best out of his brilliant cryptanalysts.

Above right: the stops and the familiar phrases that had appeared in previous 0075 messages were relatively easy to fill in. But at this point the substance of the message is still missing. One code group that long remained a mystery was the identity of 2479 (fourth line, right). Hall's sensible guess that it stood for Mexico paid off when a copy was found there.

THE ZIMMERMANN TELEGRAM PARTIALLY DECODED

0158 0075 BERLIN FOREIGN OFFICE
JANUARY 16 STOP MOST SECRET YOUR
EXCELLENCY'S PERSONAL INFORMATION
STOP TO IMPERIAL MINISTER 2479
HAND STOP 4111 0652 5310 1139 8436
1284 9088 2895 STOP 1139 8636 5731
7100 5244 8888 STOP RECEIPT
ACKNOWLEDGE STOP ZIMMERMAN STOP

the code. With more possible variations, the cryptographer can avoid making his codewords too similar.

To encode and decode, both sender and receiver must have a copy of the same code book. To make the job easier, it is desirable to use a code in which the plaintext words are listed in alphabetical order and the number groups (if numbers are used) in consecutive order. Thus, for example, if *apple* is 75976, *apple tree* might be 75977. Both the encoder and the decoder can easily refer to the same code book in order to make or to read a coded message.

Such codes, known as *one-part* codes, are sometimes useful, particularly in business, but they are easily broken. Once the code-breaker has discovered the meaning of one or two groups he can begin to make intelligent guesses. Suppose, for example, that he knows group 12345 means *ship*; when he meets the group 12346, he can guess *shipwreck*. To make codes more secure, the codegroups are applied to the plaintext words at random—either by mixing them in a hat and drawing them out at random, or by some electronic device. The encoder's book lists the words and phrases alphabetically, followed by their randomly selected number groups. As this is no use to the decoder, who must work back from the numbers, he is equipped with a book listing the words in numerical order. For example, a few consecutive entries in his book might be: "1432—*torpedo*; 1433—*agent*; 1434—*negotiated peace*." Because different books are required for encoding and decoding, this particular kind of code is called a *two-part* code.

Code 0075 was such a code. It consisted of 10,000 different groups of numbers representing, in a completely random fashion, almost as many different words and phrases.

On the morning of January 16, 1917 Montgomery was handed a message that had been intercepted on the Swedish Roundabout and he quickly recognized it as written in Code 0075. A few hours later, an identical coded message was obtained from the United States cable. Like the Swedish Roundabout intercept, it consisted of messages Nos. 157 and 158 addressed to the German ambassador Bernstorff. It did not take Montgomery and de Grey too long to identify a few familiar words, such as 4852 (*Zimmermann*) and the standard opening phrases such as 4280 (*Berlin Foreign Office*) and 5841 (*most secret*). In order to get an idea of the cable's structure, they had to fill in the stops or periods. In an elaborate code such as 0075 there are always a number of alternative groups for *stop* and for frequently used words, to prevent their being conspicuous through repetition. Often, however, the code clerk is not sufficiently cautious and will stick to very few groups. From their previous experience with Code 0075, Montgomery and de Grey were able to detect the stops in Zimmermann's telegram. With the bones of the punctuation filled in, the message began to take shape, even if its substance was still missing. The diagram opposite shows the telegram with the opening and closing phrases and the skeleton of its punctuation revealed.

Other clues to decoding any coded message in German could be found in the language itself. It is safe to assume, for example, that most groups immediately before a stop would be a verb of some kind.

After a few hours' work, Montgomery and de Grey had worked out a partial solution to this second message that, fragmentary though it was, clearly revealed political dynamite. They took it to Hall. He read the following words:

"Most secret for Your Excellency's personal information and to be handed on to the Imperial Minister in (2479) with Telegram No. 1 (. . .) by a safe route.

"We propose to begin on the 1st February unrestricted submarine warfare. In doing so, we shall endeavor to keep America neutral. (?) If we should not (succeed in doing so) we propose to (2479) an alliance upon the following basis:

"[joint] conduct of the war.

"[joint] conclusion of peace.

"(. . .)

"Your Excellency should for the present inform the President [of 2479] secretly (?that we expect) war with the USA (possibly) (. . .) (Japan) and at the same time to negotiate between us and Japan. (Please tell the President) that (. . .) or submarines (. . .) will compel England to peace in a few months. Acknowledge receipt. Zimmermann."

Above: Count Johann Heinrich von Bernstorff, German ambassador to Washington from 1908 to 1917. A popular figure in American society who genuinely wanted peace, he was appalled at the telegram and performed his part in the plot with great reluctance.

Above: a German painting of a U-boat in heavy seas picking up survivors from an Allied ship she has just sunk. Germany's resumption of unrestricted submarine warfare in 1917 helped to push the United States into the war.

On several occasions in the past, Hall had shown himself ready to act on his own initiative. Here in front of him was the lever to bring the United States into the war and save the beleaguered Allies. But the situation was not that simple. For one thing, to reveal the Zimmermann telegram to the Americans would offend the Swedes, whose cable Room 40 was not supposed to read. It would also offend the Americans, whose cables they were likewise not supposed to read. But these were minor considerations compared to the big objection: if Germany knew that the British had cracked their Code 0075, they would stop using it. Months of arduous work would have no future value. Furthermore, there was no shred of evidence that the telegram was real. It could be dismissed as a piece of propaganda.

Anxious though Hall and his superiors were to get America into the war, they knew that the United States would be unlikely to declare war before an actual attack had been made.

Above: a 1917 cartoon in the New York *Herald* shows Ambassador Bernstorff wrapped in a pirate flag with a death's head wearing a German helmet. It symbolized American belief that Germans were pirates after their decision to wage unrestricted submarine warfare.

It seemed likely that the United States would enter the war on its own initiative once the submarine attacks began. If it did not, that would be the time to reveal the Zimmermann telegram.

Hall decided to bide his time—while giving top priority to getting a word-perfect translation of the telegram. In this he was helped by the interception of Bernstorff's replies. He, poor man, had been sincere enough in wanting peace, and was outraged at Zimmermann's plans.

On February 1, as planned, the Germans began unrestricted submarine warfare. Two days later, Wilson announced to Congress that he was breaking diplomatic relations with Germany. As for a declaration of war, he would ask Congress for it only if Germany actually did attack American ships. The Allies expected this to occur within a few days.

The cryptanalysts struggled on. It was essential if the telegram

were produced that there be no unsolved words or phrases. For a cryptanalyst it is embarrassing to produce the kind of message that declares, for example, "arriving London 8674" and to have to explain that one does not know what day of the week 8674 represents.

In the Zimmermann telegram one such embarrassing gap remained: the identity of 2479, Germany's potential ally against the United States. Until 2479 was identified, the Zimmermann telegram was *Hamlet* without the prince.

Hall reviewed his priorities. It was essential to discover the meaning of 2479. It was also vital to get written proof that the telegram was real. Finally, he had to fill in the other remaining gaps so that the telegram could be presented as a stolen plaintext document and not a solution worked out by cryptanalysts. In this way, the secret of Room 40's existence could be protected.

There was one way in which all these goals could be accomplished. Hall's hunch was that 2479 was Mexico. Relations between Mexico and the United States had been severely strained in recent years, and Mexico would welcome a chance to gain back part of the southwestern United States that had once belonged to her. If, as Hall guessed, 2479 was Mexico, then Bernstorff must have sent a cable to the German ambassador

WIRE TAP

Eckhardt in Mexico City—in code, of course, but via normal commercial channels. It was probable that he would not have used Code 0075, which apparently the ambassador in Mexico did not have. If he used a code with which Room 40 was familiar, that would help the analysts to fill in the remaining gaps in the original. Moreover, Bernstorff would have had to change, if only very slightly, the wording of his version—for example, the date and the place from which it was sent. If Hall could produce this relayed version, then he might be able to convince the Germans that the telegram had been intercepted on the American continent and so conceal the workings of Room 40. Moreover, possession of the actual telegram would show without a doubt that the Zimmermann plot was for real.

Hall got in touch with an agent in Mexico City, and with his help secured from the Western Union telegraph office a copy of the telegram sent by Bernstorff to Eckhardt.

As Hall expected, the relayed Zimmermann telegram was in a different code from 0075. Bernstorff had put it into Code 13040, with which Room 40 was already familiar. This was a "hybrid" code, a mixture of the one-part type and the two-part type. In other words, code numbers had been given only a partial mixing: they had been divided into batches of 100 or so

each, and these batches had been shuffled. A decoder could count on having a good quantity of numbers in strict sequence to match against alphabetically arranged words.

Combining their knowledge of Code 13040 with their almost complete solution of the original telegram in 0075, the cryptanalysts were able to give Hall a complete text of the Zimmermann telegram as relayed by Bernstorff to Eckhardt. Still Hall waited, hoping that the United States would enter the war on its own initiative. There were no overt acts by the Germans against the United States, and so no declaration of war from the American government. Meanwhile, the Allies grew more desperate.

On February 22, three weeks after the German announcement of unrestricted submarine warfare, Hall—with the approval of the Foreign Office—took the telegram to Edward Bell, a contact of his who worked for the American embassy in London, and the two of them showed it to Ambassador Page. For Page, who had long been anxious for his country to take the plunge, the telegram was as welcome as it was shocking.

Page's immediate task was to send the telegram's contents to the State Department and the president, along with a covering letter explaining how it had been obtained. Hall helped him with this letter, deftly concealing the real story of Room 40's eavesdropping and decoding activities. According to Page's note, the British had obtained the German Code 13040 early in the war and had also intercepted communications between Bernstorff and Eckhardt. "This accounts for their being able to decipher this telegram," he explained.

The bombshell had the desired effect. The appalled President Wilson was even more indignant when a State Department official discovered, among the department's files, a copy of the original telegram sent by Zimmermann to Bernstorff. The Germans' effrontery in using the American diplomatic cable to offer part of the United States to Mexico staggered the president.

After some discussion as to how to proceed, Wilson agreed to Secretary of State Lansing's plan to release the document to the press. On March 1, Zimmermann's telegram splashed across the front pages of American newspapers. The House of Representatives passed by 403 to 13 a bill to arm merchant ships. But the Senate remained skeptical, wondering if the telegram was an elaborate plot on the part of the Allies to bring the United States into the war. As a further check, the State Department managed to get hold of another copy of Bernstorff's telegram from Western Union—despite a federal law protecting the privacy of telegrams. They sent this to Page in London, apologetically asking if someone in the United States embassy could obtain permission from the British to see a copy of the code and decode the message. Edward Bell went to the Admiralty where he was shown Code 13040 and decoded the first few words of the telegram himself, before turning the rest of the job over to Nigel de Grey.

Above: President Woodrow Wilson, an academic who entered politics in his 50s and attained the country's highest office in 1913. After being reelected in 1916 on the slogan of having "kept America out of the war," he was forced by events to enter the conflict in 1917. After the war he strove hard to involve the United States in the League of Nations to preserve the peace, but Congress opposed him and would not approve membership in it. Wilson suffered a complete nervous collapse, from which he never recovered, as a result of this disappointment.

In the meantime, the Germans were busily trying to discover the source of the leak. They gave Eckhardt a slow roasting. They assumed, as the British trusted they would, that the telegram had been "lifted" in his office. The poor man defended himself in earnest humility: any telegrams, including this one, he stressed, were read to him in a low voice in his private quarters by his secretary. There were no carbons, and the original of any secret telegram was burned. There was no way, he insisted, in which the telegram could have been stolen. Room 40 eavesdropped on these exchanges with great glee.

All kinds of stories circulated as to how the United States government had obtained the telegram. Articles in the British press, crediting the Americans with its discovery and complaining at the inefficiency of the British Secret Service, must have provoked a few ironic smiles in Room 40.

Below: a painting of American soldiers embarking at Southampton, England, on their way to France. The arrival of American troops in Europe helped to tip the balance in favor of the Allies and make possible the eventual victory.

Above: Mata Hari. A spy for the Germans, she was of Dutch birth and her real name was Gertrud Margarete Zelle. Information obtained by Room 40 helped in capturing her.

Right: a painting of the Battle of Jutland. A series of human errors prevented the British Navy from achieving the victory it was expecting.

The Successes of Room 40

By the middle of 1916, two years into World War I, the cryptanalysts of the British Admiralty had become the most efficient code-breakers in the world. Working unobtrusively in Room 40, their modest headquarters, they got so fast at solving the Germans' codes that they often mastered the new ones within two hours, and rarely took longer than 10 hours. This was particularly remarkable in view of the fact that the Germans changed ciphers almost daily.

There were many instances in which the intelligence from Room 40 affected wartime decisions and events favorably. The Battle of Jutland, however, was a disappointment for the British. It was hoped that a victory would give them absolute mastery of the North Sea. But the naval encounter ended as a stand-off. Was it a failure on the part of Room 40 intelligence? The facts prove it was not.

The Germans planned to lure the British Grand Fleet out into the open for an attack by submarines and their High Seas Fleet. However, the strategy was to assault only a section of the British Fleet in order to avoid a general engagement. All this was known to Room 40 within hours, and was relayed to Admiral Sir John Jellicoe with dispatch.

This is when human error tipped the advantage away from the British. Through oversight, Admiral Jellicoe was not told that the call-sign of the German flagship had been changed, and he naturally assumed that the High Seas Fleet was still in port. Instead, he met the German naval forces in the middle of the North Sea. This shook his faith in the reliability of Room 40 intelligence.

His distrust deepened when he later plotted the position of the German cruiser *Regensburg* as given by the Admiralty. He found that it would have been in the same spot

his own ship was in if the Admiralty information were correct. What he could not possibly know was that the *Regensburg* navigator had made a 10-mile error in his calculations, and the error lay with him rather than with Room 40's deciphering.

But the damage was done. When the Admiralty sent him the next message about the position of the High Seas Fleet—which, incidentally, Room 40 had deciphered in less than one hour—he withdrew instead of attacking on the basis of information he could not trust. The chance for a victory was lost.

On the other hand, the story of the capture of Sir Roger Casement is an example of how Room 40 intelligence was used to full advantage. Casement, a former British Consul, was an Irish patriot who tried to get German support for an Irish rebellion while the war was on. Messages flew back and forth between Berlin and German diplomatic posts in the still neutral USA.

Room 40 found out that if a cable was sent with the codeword OATS in it, Casement would be landing in Ireland from a German submarine; the word HAY in the cable would mean that he was not aboard that time. On April 12, 1916 a cable appeared with the codeword OATS. Ten days later Casement was arrested as he came ashore in Ireland. Three months later he was convicted of high treason and hanged.

It was also owing to Room 40 intelligence that the French caught the most famous female spy of World War I, Mata Hari. Room 40 intercepted diplomatic messages in code from Madrid to Berlin in which the German naval attaché asked for funds and instructions for the exotic spy. Ordered to Paris, she was arrested by authorities who had had the benefit of the information decoded by Room 40. The luckless Mata Hari was convicted and shot.

Below: the Irish patriot Roger Casement, who was captured by the British as a result of Room 40's cryptanalytic work.

Above: a field radio set being used in the trenches during World War I. Radio signals made communication easier than by telegraph, but they also helped the code-breakers

Any remaining doubts as to the telegram's authenticity disappeared when Zimmermann himself, to everyone's astonishment, confessed, "I cannot deny it. It is true."

Psychologically, Zimmermann's plan was precisely the kind of plot to incite the Americans to war. Those Americans, particularly in the West and Southwest, who had felt remote from the war in Europe and to some extent indifferent to it now faced the alarming possibility of attack on their own borders. The foreign war had suddenly become an American war. President Wilson, who had been reelected to keep the nation at peace, now went to Congress to tell them that the "intercepted note to the German minister in Mexico City is eloquent evidence. We are accepting this challenge of hostile purpose." Congress passed the declaration of war. The work of the civil servants in Room 40 had paid off.

The arrival of American troops in France made possible the winning of the war—but by no means immediately. By 1918, the impact of their presence was more than countered by the return to the Western Front of 3 million German soldiers who were no longer needed to fight the Russians, who had made a separate peace with Germany.

The Allies guessed correctly that Germany planned to launch an offensive in the spring, in a last desperate attempt to capture Paris before the arrival of more Americans would once more tip the scales against them. What the Allies did not know was at what point along the Front the attack would come. In order to thwart the offensive, the Allies would have to mass their forces at the right spot—wherever that might be. In such circumstances the interception and decoding of German messages became of crucial importance.

For their part, the Germans recognized the urgency of a new code or cipher to protect the secrecy of their plan. Throughout the conflict, German security had taken more than a few hammerings. This was partly due to the widespread use of radio to send messages.

Radio communication opened up new possibilities for cryptanalysts. Whereas messages sent by hand were rarely intercepted and messages sent by telegraph could be obtained only by physically tapping the line, radio signals go through the air for anyone to hear. The sheer volume of communications sent by radio during World War I meant that cryptanalysts had much more material to work with, and so more opportunities to crack the enemy's codes and ciphers.

Even when the signals could not be deciphered, they could give away valuable information by their volume and direction. The French, whose intelligence service was already well-organized before the war, quickly became adept at such "traffic analysis," and their radio receiving stations, situated along the length of the Front, enabled them to get a fairly clear picture of the German forces and their distribution. They could guess with a fair amount of confidence that a sudden increase in messages

Above: a drawing of a radio operator on board a British trawler during World War I. The volume and direction of messages were valuable clues in plotting their source.

Above: the Eiffel Tower was of great importance to France during the war. From the top of the tower, 984 feet high, radio signals could be transmitted as far as southern Africa and South America (as shown on the upside-down map in this drawing). The tower was also equipped with sensitive receiving apparatus capable of picking up radio messages sent to the German Army from headquarters in Berlin.

from a particular transmitter would be followed by some activity by the forces nearest that station. A change in the location of a transmitter could yield clues. Suppose, for example, that a message in a particular cipher was transmitted by a Commandant Schmidt (often the signature was in plaintext) from Gravelotte and that on the following day another message from Schmidt was transmitted from Pont-à-Mousson, some 20 miles away. From the speed of the movement, one could infer that Schmidt's unit was cavalry or horse-drawn artillery rather than infantry.

The French cryptanalysts had a talent for intuition and initiative. If, for example, they suspected that a particular code-group, say 10357, might stand for *tanks*, they might send out some French tanks as a diversionary exercise within sight of the enemy transmitter. Then they would listen to the signals to see if the sighting of French 10357 would be reported.

The Germans had at first been rather careless in their use of ciphers. They would, for example, test out a new one by enciphering a proverb in it, and once the French became aware of this practice, they could crack the cipher by trying various

German proverbs against the test message until one fitted. The German tendency to use patriotic words such as *Fatherland* or *Kaiser* as keys to cipher messages also simplified the work of the French cryptanalysts.

Despite their apparent variety, all ciphers fall into three basic categories: substitution ciphers, transposition ciphers, and combinations of these two types. A simple example of a substitution cipher is one devised and used for a short time by Julius Caesar. For each letter in the plaintext he substituted the third letter farther on in the alphabet. Thus, using the present-day 26-letter alphabet, the word *legions* would be enciphered OHJLRQV. In a transposition cipher, the letters of the plaintext are scrambled, according to some system. Thus, the letters of the word *legions*, if rearranged in reverse alphabetical order, could form *sonlige*. Combining the two systems, we could transpose the substituted letters to get VRQOLJH. From these fundamental principles, ciphers of great complexity can be devised.

Besides the general system of a cipher—the agreed basic series of steps known to both the sender and the receiver of the message—there is usually a *key*—a special word, phrase, or group of numbers that can be changed at will to enhance security.

The ADFGX Cipher

To ensure secrecy for his projected spring offensive, General Ludendorff demanded a new cipher, sufficiently complex to baffle the French cryptanalysts until Paris could be captured. The cipher ultimately chosen was devised by Fritz Nebel, a radio staff officer in the German Army's headquarters near Mainz. One of its advantages was ease of transmission. By 1918 the Germans had some 15,000 operators along the Front, many of them inadequately trained. Nebel's cipher used just five letters—A, D, F, G, and X—which, in Morse code, are easily distinguishable from each other and so less likely to be confused by either the sender or the receiver.

Having decided to restrict the cipher text to those five letters, Nebel then had to devise a system in which the combinations of the letters could be substituted for the letters of the alphabet in a plaintext message. His solution was both elegant and simple. He drew a grid (shown opposite) in which the letters of the alphabet (only 25, as there is no Y in German) were arranged at random five across and five down, with *adfgx* along the top and the left side. To encipher the letter *c* for example, the sender would signal first G, from the side, and then F, from the top. Both the sender and the receiver would know the basic arrangement. The arrangement of the alphabet within the square could be changed as often as necessary.

Thus far, Nebel was using a device centuries old, named the *Polybius square* for the Greek writer who invented it. Also known as the *grid*, or *checkerboard*, the square translates letters

Left: German Field Marshal Ludendorff (left) planning strategy. It was essential for the Germans to launch an offensive in the spring of 1918 before the Allied forces received sufficient American reinforcements to give them numerical superiority.

Below: the ADFGX cipher devised by Fritz Nebel for use by the Germans is one of the most famous field ciphers in all of cryptology. In the first stage of encipherment the message is transposed into paired letters, always working from the side to the top of the checkerboard table. The first letter of the message, *Forced to retreat*, lies in the fifth column, the third letter down. Reading from the side first gives F, and reading the top next gives X, so the paired letters for *f* will be FX.

THE ADFGX CHECKERBOARD AND FIRST STAGE IN ENCIPHERING

	A	D	F	G	X
A	n	b	x	r	u
D	q	o	k	d	v
F	a	h	s	g	f
G	m	z	c	l	t
X	e	i	p	j	w

FX DD AG GF XA DG GX DD AG XA GX AG XA FA GX

f o r c e d t o r e t r e a t

of a plaintext into numbers or into a limited number of alternative letters. Polybius saw the grid's usefulness as a means of signaling over distances: five flashes with the left hand, two with the right, and so on.

In terms of security, however, the grid by itself has little value. A message (above right) in which the letters have simply been replaced with two-letter equivalents can easily be deciphered. For one thing, the message is in its original order of letters. For another, the equivalent for any letter remains constant. One of the basic tools of any cryptanalyst is a knowledge of the relative frequency with which different letters occur in a language. Equipped with this information, the cryptana-

Right: in the second stage of encipherment the message is written in horizontal rows across a given number of columns—in this case 20—without pairing the letters. The numbers are scrambled, and it is these scrambled numbers that become the transposition key. In the first stage the word *forced* had become FX DD AG GF XA DG. Notice that these letters are now the first 12 of the first row, in columns not numbered in any sequence.

Right: in the final encipherment stage the message is written in five-letter groups taken from the numbered rows in order—that is, FADXF comes from the row marked 1, and XAXFD from 2. However, because row 2 has only four letters in it, the fifth letter is taken from the top of row 3, the next one in sequence.

THE ADFGX CIPHER — TRANSPOSITION KEY

8	9	14	7	19	13	16	1	15	6	3	10	17	2	20	5	11	18	4	12
F	X	D	D	A	G	G	F	X	A	D	G	G	X	D	D	A	G	X	A
G	X	A	G	X	A	F	A	G	X	G	X	X	A	A	A	D	F	G	A
G	X	D	D	F	A	A	D	A	D	X	A	D	X	X	D	G	G	G	G
X	A	F	X	X	A	X	X	G	F	F	A	F	F	A	X	F	A	G	G
G	X	X	D	X	A	F	F												

Message: Forced to retreat ten km to Abbeville few casualties

THE ADFGX CIPHER — COMPLETED TRANSPOSITION

FADXF XAXFD GXFXG GGDAD XAXDF DGDXD

FGGXG XXXAX GXAAA DGFAA GGGAA AADAD

FXXGA GGFAX FGXDF GFGAA XFXXD AXA

lyst can swiftly get inside a cipher based on substitution alone.

The average frequency of letters in a 195-letter sample of written English is as follows:

16	3	6	8	21	4	3	12	13	I	I	7	6
A	B	C	D	E	F	G	H	I	J	K	L	M

14	16	4	$\frac{1}{2}$	13	12	18	6	2	3	I	4	$\frac{1}{2}$
N	O	P	Q	R	S	T	U	V	W	X	Y	Z

Such frequency tables are based on samples of text millions of letters long. The actual frequency of letters within a short sample will vary from these averages, but will conform enough so that the cryptanalyst can make some intelligent guesses. He also uses his knowledge of letter combinations within a language. For example, TH is a common grouping in English, and SCH occurs often in German. Once he discovers that the plaintext letter *n* is represented by the cipher letter P, he can be fairly certain that four times out of five—in English—the letter in front of P will be a vowel. He can usually identify plaintext *e* fairly quickly, as it is the commonest letter (in German and French as well as in English), and he can usually then go on to identify the next most frequent vowels, *a, i,* and *o*, which seldom appear together. Armed with these and many other language characteristics, the cryptanalyst is able to proceed with the trial and error substitution process known as *anagraming*. He tries out and then discards one hypothesis after another until the shape of the message emerges and he can identify the remaining letters simply from his knowledge of the words themselves. To the layman the anagraming process may sound exceedingly complicated, but to a cryptanalyst it is easy and pleasant work.

If the French had had only Nebel's basic substitution grid to contend with, they would have solved it in minutes. But Nebel devised ingenious ways of disguising his letter pairs, which were to baffle the French cryptanalysts right up to the 11th hour.

Having completed a substitution process, Nebel then passed the cipher through a transposition process. Its purpose was to "encipher the cipher" or *superencipher* it—in other words, to rearrange the coded message so that the tell-tale frequencies would no longer be apparent. There are a number of ways in which Colonel Nebel might have done this.

The method he chose used a numerical key, a sequence of numbers from 1 through 20 arranged in a scrambled order, that could be changed as often as necessary. The letter pairs were broken up and listed singly under the numbers, still from left to right, as seen opposite (top). The key could be changed as often as necessary. The transposition was achieved by writing the letters in the order of their vertical arrangement under the key numbers. As a further disguise, they were arranged in groups of five. This meant that the letter pairs would often be split between one group and the next (as shown opposite).

On receiving a message, the decoder could quickly establish the depth of the numbered columns by dividing the number of letters in the message by 20, the number of columns. The odd number left over—in this case 6—would be the number of letters in the bottom, incomplete line. Once he had filled in his vertical columns, he could read the letter pairs from left to right and then substitute the plaintext letters for them according to that day's substitution key—that is, the arrangement of the alphabet within the grid.

Nebel later observed that he would have been happier to see his cipher given a double transposition—that is, another scrambling on top of the first one. But the chiefs of radiography and decipherment argued that a further complication would make communication too slow. A daily change of the substitution and transposition keys was deemed adequate for security. For some time this judgment seemed correct.

On March 5, 1918, French radio receivers picked up the first signals in Cipher ADFGX. They knew that the strange new patterns must signal a new development in German strategy—probably the start of the long-dreaded spring offensive.

The messages in the new cipher—like those in previous ciphers—were sent to the Bureau du Chiffre in Paris. There, they were given to Captain Georges Painvin, a paleontologist and a brilliant cellist who also had a genius for cryptanalysis. For the next three and a half months Painvin wrestled with the most daunting and exhausting task of his life.

Above: Fritz Nebel, photographed in 1974, looks through a photo album of his days in the army during World War I. The picture he shows is the one of himself on page 54.

Above: German troops going "over the top" of the trenches. The last big German offensive began on March 21, 1918. Two months later they were only 50 miles from Paris.

Confronted with the first ADFGX message, he had little trouble guessing that a checkerboard lay behind it. Only by such an arrangement could the five letters substitute for all of the letters of the alphabet. He could also guess that both the arrangement of the letters in the checkerboard and some other key (the row numbers) were being regularly changed.

For the first few weeks Painvin was hampered in his work by the scarcity of messages in the new cipher. He simply did not have enough material to work with. However, traffic analysis had established the fact that the few messages intercepted were sent from a point far behind the Front, which meant the German High Command stations.

On March 21 the Germans began their offensive. Opening with the most furious burst of gunfire since the beginning of the war, they proceeded to break through a 40-mile section of the Front and, within a week, to push the Allies back as far as Amiens, a distance of 38 miles.

On the move, the Germans had to rely more heavily on radio communications than on the telegraph, which had served them in trench warfare. The relative ease of intercepting these radio messages produced more material for Painvin. Even so, it was not enough, and as the Germans continued their advance, Painvin struggled on at what seemed a hopeless task.

Then, on April 1, the French intercepted 18 messages in Cipher ADFGX, and Painvin made a breakthrough. He noted

CHI-110:	(1) ADXDA	(2) XGFXG	(3) DAXXGX	(4) GDADFF	(5) GXDAG
CHI-104:	(1) ADXDD	(2) XGFFD	(3) DAXAGD	(4) GDGXD	(5) GXDFG
CHI-110:	(6) AGFFFD	(7) XGDDGA	(8) DFADG	(9) AAFFGX	(10) DDDXD
CHI-104:	(6) AGAAXG	(7) GXG?D	(8) DFADG	(9) AAFFF	(10) DDDFF
CHI-110:	(11) DGXAXA	(12) DXFFD	(13) DXFAG	(14) XGGAGA	(15) GFGFF
CHI-104:	(11) DGDGF	(12) DXXXA	(13) DXFDAF	(14) XGGAGF	(15) GFGXX
CHI-110:	(16) AGXXDD	(17) AGGFD	(18) AADXFX	(19) ADFGXD	(20) AAXAG
CHI-104:	(16) AGXXA	(17) AGGAA	(18) AADAFF	(19) ADFFG	(20) AAFFA

CIPHERS 104 AND 110 COMPARED   STAGE 2

(1)	(2)	(3)	(4)	(5)	(6)	(7)	(8)	(9)	(10)	(11)	(12)	(13)	(14)	(15)	(16)	(17)	(18)	(19)	(20)
AA	XX	DD	GG	GG	AA	XG	DD	AA	DD	DD	DD	DD	XX	GG	AA	AA	AA	AA	AA
DD	GG	AA	DD	XX	GG	GX	FF	AA	DD	GG	XX	XX	GG	FF	GG	GG	AA	DD	AA
XX	FF	XX	AG	DD	FA	DG	AA	FF	DD	XD	FX	FF	GG	GG	XX	GG	DD	FF	XF
DD	XF	XA	DX	AF	FA	D?	DD	FF	XF	AG	FX	AD	AA	FX	XX	FA	XA	GF	AF
AD	GD	GG	FD	GG	FX	GD	GG	GF	DF	XF	DA	GA	GG	FX	DA	DA	FF	XG	GA
	XD	F		DG	A		X		A		F	AF		D			XF	D	

that the opening sections of two messages (which he called CHI-110 and CHI-104) had certain similarities, which became even more striking when he arranged the five-letter groups in vertical order (see the diagrams above). Moreover, when the groups were arranged in this way, their varying length—some five letters long, some six letters long—gave Painvin an important clue. Both messages in their original form—that is, after letter substitution but before the transposition of the columns—must have ended with short lines. Painvin reasoned correctly that the long columns containing two letters would have been on the left; those containing one letter (from the longer CHI-110) somewhere in the middle; and the short columns at the right. He now had a rough guide to the transposition key. By repeating the same process on the end of the message he was able to establish the order of columns a little more precisely. The remaining 16 messages intercepted on April 1 gave him more material to divide into columns and to analyze. Through a tedious process of rearranging columns and making frequency counts of the letter pairs produced through various combinations, he was finally able to establish the identity of the letter *e*, which was DG.

Much more work remained to be done before the other letters could be identified. In all, the task took Painvin four days and four nights. Even then, of course, he had solved the substitution and transposition keys for only one day—April 1, 1918—but at

Above: the first breakthrough made by Georges Painvin in his efforts to crack the cipher. He noticed that some messages started with the same letters—as seen in messages CHI-110 and CHI-104 at the top—and decided that such identical fragments could represent identical tops of columns of a transposition table. When he aligned the letters vertically—as in Stage 2—he saw the possibility of the paired letters. The variation in column length was a clue as to the approximate positions of the columns before they had been transposed on a table.

least he now knew in essence how the German system worked.

For nearly two months there was a dearth of ADFGX intercepts. Then on May 27, with a new German offensive, more telegrams arrived on Painvin's desk. As Painvin labored at his task, the Germans advanced to within 50 miles of Paris. In the capital one could occasionally hear the gunfire at the Front. By now, however, American troops were arriving in great numbers; and their efforts had helped to check the German advance. The Germans knew that their final push must be made soon, before the American strength increased much further and turned the odds against them.

The ADFGVX Cipher

At this critical moment, Painvin had, as he later recalled, "the agony, which I shall never forget, of seeing substituted for the five-letter telegrams, ADFGX, six-letter telegrams ADFGVX."

The Germans had added V to the checkerboard in order to make possible encipherment of numbers. With the five-letter cipher, numbers had had to be spelled out; the addition of V created new letter pairs, so that the numerals 0 through 9 could be included in the checkerboard.

Within 24 hours, Painvin managed to figure out the significance of the new addition to the cipher. But in the meantime, a more baffling puzzle faced the generals: at which point along the Front would the Germans make their final offensive? There were five probable locations: Flanders, Amiens, Compiègne, Reims, and Verdun. At which of these points should the Allies concentrate their forces? The fate of Paris and of the nation hung on their decision. The suspense was almost unbearable—not least in the office where Painvin made his way through the labyrinth of ADFGVX in search of some clue to the German plans.

On June 1 more than 70 telegrams arrived. Painvin began sifting through them, and in a relatively short time he found two that—like CHI-110 and CHI-104—had identical sections. Concentrating on these two telegrams, he succeeded in breaking both the substitution and the transposition keys for June 1. Now he could proceed to decipher the remaining telegrams.

Among them he found a short one from the German High Command to a point on the Front near Compiègne. Painvin went to work on it, and soon deciphered the message. It read (translated into English): "RUSH MUNITIONS STOP BY DAY TOO IF NOT SEEN."

This brief message, later called by the French "Le Télégramme de la Victoire," pinpointed the area where the attack would take place. Aerial reconnaissance confirmed the news. The French, British, and Americans reinforced the Front at Compiègne and waited tensely for the attack. On June 9 it came. The Allies at first fell back; but on the third day they hit

Above: Georges Painvin today, with some of the labyrinthine calculations he made in his struggle to crack the cipher. He says that he still finds satisfaction in the memory of his successful work, achieved at great cost to his well-being.

LE TELEGRAMME DE LA VICTOIRE—SUBSTITUTION KEY

	A	D	F	G	V	X
A	c	o	8	x	f	4
D	m	k	3	a	z	9
F	n	w	l	0	j	d
G	5	s	i	y	h	u
V	p	l	v	b	6	r
X	e	q	7	t	2	g

LE TELEGRAMME DE LA VICTOIRE—TRANSPOSITION KEY

6	16	7	5	17	2	14	10	15	9	13	1	21	12	4	8	19	3	11	20	18
D	A	G	X	F	A	G	F	X	G	G	F	A	D	F	A	G	F	X	A	V
X	G	X	F	A	X	X	V	G	X	A	G	D	A	A	G	V	F	F	X	A
G	X	F	A	G	F	X	X	X	A	F	A	V	A	G	X	F	A	D	D	X
G	G	D	A	D	F	D	X	A	G	F	X	G	F	A	G	F	A	A	G	V
X	G	X	A	G	F	F	A	X	X	X	A	G	D	X	A	G	V	X	A	F
A	D	G	G	X	A	A	G	V	V	G	X	A	G	F	X	G	D	G	X	X

LE TELEGRAMME DE LA VICTOIRE DECIPHERED

DA	GX	FA	GF	XG	GF	AD	FA	GF	XA	VX	GX	FA	XX
M	u	n	i	t	i	o	n	i	e	r	u	n	g

VG	XA	GD	AA	GV	FF	XA	GX	FA	GF	XX	XA	FA	VA
b	e	s	c	h	l	e	u	n	i	g	e	n	P

GX	FA	DD	XG	GD	AD	FD	XA	GF	XG	FA	GF	AA	GV
u	n	k	t	s	o	w	e	i	t	n	i	c	h

XG	XA	GF	FA	XX	XA	GD	XA	GV	XA	FA	DG	GX	AA
t	e	i	n	g	e	s	e	h	e	n	a	u	c

GV	VG	XA	GF	XG	DG	XX
h	b	e	i	T	a	g

Left: stages in deciphering the crucial telegram that revealed where the Germans intended to launch the final part of their offensive. Once Painvin had figured out the substitution key for the day (V had now been added to the cipher) and the transposition key, he was able to rearrange the columns in their original order and convert the letter pairs into their plaintext equivalents. Translated into English, the message reads: "Rush munitions stop by day too if not seen." It had been sent to the Front at Compiègne. This information provided by Painvin enabled the Allies to concentrate their forces where they were needed and so thwart the offensive and save Paris.

the Germans with a savage bombardment that put an end to the German advance toward Paris. The war was to last another six months, but the tide had been turned.

As for Painvin, whose grueling labors had made possible the counterattack at Compiègne and the saving of Paris, he was physically exhausted. He had lost 33 pounds, sitting at his desk. He spent a period of six months in the hospital recuperating from his experience. And yet, harrowing as that experience had been, he later recalled it with some satisfaction. His solutions of the ADFGVX intercepts, he said, left "an indelible mark on my spirit and remain for me one of the brightest and most outstanding memories of my existence."

World War II: PURPLE
4

Toward noon one warm Sunday in December on the Hawaiian island of Oahu, telegram delivery boy Tadao Fuchikama was weaving his motorbike through the snarled-up traffic on his way to the U.S. Army base of Fort Shafter. He carried a message addressed to its Commanding General.

Normally on a Sunday he would have arrived at the base long before then. But around Pearl Harbor it had not been a normal Sunday. Thick palls of oily smoke still obscured the blue skies, hours after the Japanese planes had unloaded their cargo of death on the American ships lying at anchor. Tadao might have been excused for not completing his rounds under such chaotic circumstances. But he had continued stoically on his way, twice being stopped by National Guardsmen suspicious that the uniformed Japanese-Hawaiian might be a paratrooper.

He had no notion, of course, of the contents of the coded message that he carried. As he delivered it to the officer at Fort Shafter he could not have guessed that it was the first warning from Washington to Pearl Harbor that Japan might be planning an attack—the very attack that had taken place that morning.

By 2:40 p.m. the telegram had finally been decoded. It was from General George C. Marshall, Chief of Staff, and it revealed that the Japanese were going to deliver an ultimatum to the U.S. government at 1:00 p.m. Washington time (8:00 a.m. Hawaii time). "Just what significance the hour set may have we do not know," the message concluded, "but be on alert accordingly." General Short glanced over the message and immediately threw it into the wastebasket.

A little before 8:00 a.m. that Sunday, the men of the Pacific Fleet had been at breakfast. The sound of church bells from Honolulu wafted over the harbor. The local radio station played languorous melodies of the islands. Some 45 minutes earlier, two army privates stationed at the north tip of Oahu had spotted on a radar screen a large blip about 140 miles from the island and decided it must be a flight of planes. They reported it to their superior, but he and his fellow officers concluded that it must be American planes. The privates were told to "forget it."

The ferocity of the attack, when it came, was something new in warfare. Fifty high-level bombers, 70 torpedo bombers, 51

Above: the U.S. battleship *California* in flames during the Japanese attack on Pearl Harbor, December 7, 1941. The surprise attack, which brought America into World War II, was launched before the Japanese embassy could decode and deliver Tokyo's warning to the United States. Right: an Italian postcard shows a Samurai warrior, flanked by Axis flags, destroying the Allied fleets.

dive bombers, and 43 fighters hammered down on Pearl Harbor and the crowded ranks of "Battleship Row." One of the bombs plunged straight down the stack of the battleship *Arizona*, blowing the ship to pieces and killing 1000 of her crew. The *Oklahoma*, split apart by three torpedoes, rolled over to settle upside down, only her keel visible above water. The men who managed to leap from her as she went were machine-gunned by the fighter pilots as they swam. The *West Virginia* was sunk. Five other battleships—the *California*, *Maryland*, *Nevada*, *Pennsylvania*, and *Tennessee*—were also badly damaged. By 8:30, when the first wave of the attack was over, there was hardly a vessel in the harbor not sunk or listing. For a few moments the skies were clear of planes, although few survivors noticed the lull in the continuing din of explosions, sirens, and antiaircraft fire. Then the second wave hit the island: 170 more Japanese planes swooped down upon their prey. When the attack was finally over, nearly two hours after it began, the United States had lost 349 aircraft, 18 warships, and 3700 servicemen, officers, and civilians. The Japanese had lost 29 aircraft and 55 men.

As the Japanese had intended, the Americans had been taken completely by surprise. It was an act unprecedented in the history of civilized nations. Article I of the Hague Convention, governing the conduct of war and signed in 1907, stipulated that "... hostilities ... must not commence without previous and explicit warning, in the form of a reasoned declaration of war or of an ultimatum with conditional declaration of war." The Japanese had, in fact, prepared such an ultimatum and had planned to deliver it approximately half an hour before the attack, in time to fulfill, technically, the "previous warning" condition but too late to give the Americans a chance to prepare any defense. In the event, the ultimatum was not delivered until after 2:00 p.m., well after the attack, when news of it was just reaching Washington.

At that time, the Japanese ambassador Nomura and his associate Kurusu were admitted to the office of Secretary of State Cordell Hull. They handed him a lengthy document from their government. Hull glanced through it, pretending to read it, then he looked Nomura straight in the eye. "In all my 50 years of public service," he said, "I have never seen a document that was more crowded with infamous falsehoods and distortions— infamous falsehoods and distortions on a scale so huge that I never imagined until today that any government on this planet was capable of uttering them." Curtly, he nodded toward the door, and the ambassador silently withdrew.

Hull had had good reason to give the ultimatum only a casual glance: *he had already read it*. In one of the most extraordinary feats of code-breaking in history, United States cryptanalysts had intercepted and broken the top-secret message *before* its Japanese recipients at the embassy had done so. How this had happened makes one of the most dramatic stories of World War II.

Above: a photograph captured from the Japanese shows an aerial view of the Pearl Harbor attack. At the center a plane soars upward after a direct hit on a battleship.

Right: the attack seen from the ground. Flame and smoke cover the Naval Air Station. Two thirds of American naval aircraft were destroyed, and only 16 usable Army Air Force bombers remained after the attack on Pearl Harbor.

To be sure, the American code-breakers had not managed to warn their government of the attack, but this was for a very good reason: no message containing this information had been sent. And out in the Pacific, the Japanese striking force had moved stealthily nearer and nearer its target under cover of total radio silence, so that even traffic analysis was impossible. Against such obstacles the most skilled cryptanalysts in the world would be helpless. The remarkable thing was that the United States had acquired a code-breaking establishment capable of penetrating their adversary's most secret cipher and of helping to make possible several significant victories during the war.

William Frederick Friedman

The closing of Yardley's black chamber in 1929 had temporarily put a stop to the State Department's involvement in the reading of other nations' mail, but it certainly did not put a stop to the practice itself. Even before the chamber was disbanded, its successor had been created. This was the Signal Intelligence Service—part of the U.S. Army's Signal Corps—whose stated purpose was to prepare codes and ciphers for the army, to intercept and solve the enemy's communications during wartime, and to conduct training and research in peacetime. Its small staff was headed by a man who became America's greatest cryptanalyst, William Frederick Friedman.

He had been born Wolfe Friedman in Russia, in 1891, and had come to America with his family while still an infant. His father spoke eight languages and had worked in Russia as an interpreter for the post office. Young William soon showed that he too was intellectually gifted. An honor student at his high school in Pittsburg, he went on to study genetics at Cornell University. Soon after entering graduate school he was lured away to a job as a geneticist for a wealthy textile merchant and farm owner, George Fabyan.

Fabyan was one of those people intent on proving that Shakespeare's plays were written by Bacon, and on his 500-acre estate he had set up a Department of Ciphers, with a staff of about 15, who pored over Elizabethan manuscripts in an effort to find proof of the Baconian theory. Friedman soon got diverted from his genetic work into the work of the cipher department.

One of his associates was a young woman named Elizebeth Smith (spelled with an *e* by her mother to avoid the short form Eliza). Friedman and Miss Smith soon found themselves more and more attracted not only to cryptology but also to each other. In 1917 they married; and so began, in the words of David Kahn, "the most famous husband and wife team in the history of cryptology."

Fabyan's private establishment in Riverbank, Illinois—dedicated as it was to following tortuous and probably blind alleys of literary research—might seem an unlikely group to

Above: William Frederick Friedman, America's most brilliant cryptanalyst, who established the army's Signal Intelligence Service in 1930.

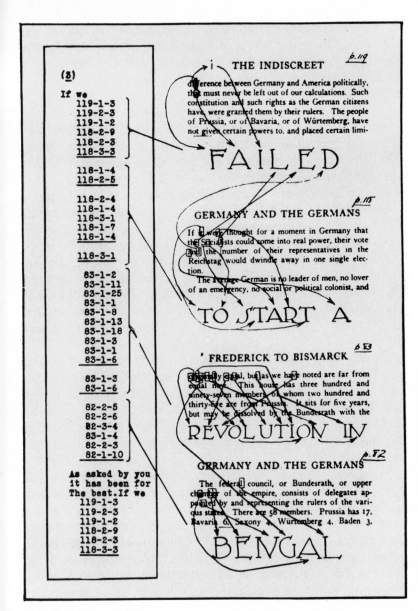

Left: an excerpt from a seven-page letter consisting mostly of numbers, which was sent by an Indian conspirator to a co-conspirator in Germany. The writer used a book—entitled *Germany and the Germans*—as his source, and enciphered the letters of his plaintext according to the page, line, and position of the letter in that line (the first, second, and third numbers in each group). William Friedman was able to break the cipher and reconstruct some parts of the passages from which the letters had been taken, even though he did not know which book the encoder had used.

become involved in an international plot. Yet by the time America entered World War I in 1917 the Riverbank staff were sufficiently skilled for the government to give them occasional intercepts to solve. (Yardley's MI8 was not yet established.) Some of these intercepts concerned one of the more bizarre sideshows of the war: the attempt by a ring of 125 Asian Indians to start an uprising against British rule—with the help of Germany—while the British were preoccupied with the war in Europe.

Intercepted messages between the Germans and the Indians, who were planning to purchase arms for the uprising in the United States, were sent to Riverbank for decipherment. Friedman, who was now chief of the cipher department, tackled the Indians' messages and soon cracked their cipher. The Indians were brought to trial in Chicago and San Francisco, and

Below: this photo of a page from a Japanese code book of the early 1930s was sent to the U.S. State Department by a person named Momose, who tried, without success, to sell the codes to the USA.

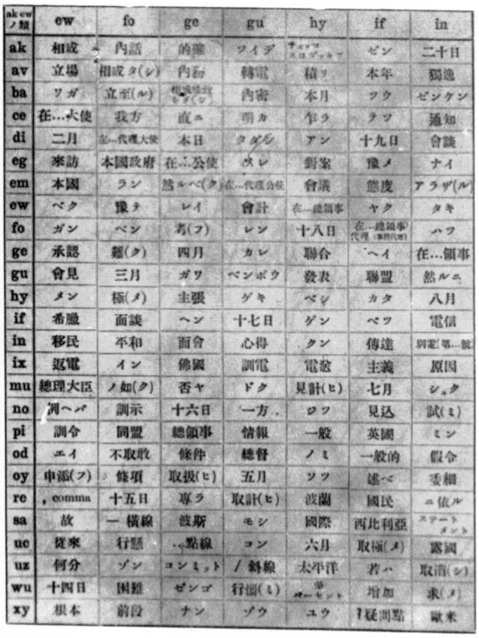

ak ew ノ組	ew	fo	ge	gu	hy	if	in
ak	相成	內話	的確	ツイデ	チェッコスロヴァキア	ゼン	二十日
av	立場	相成タ(シ)	內務	轉電	積リ	本年	獨逸
ba	ソガ	立至(ル)	[illegible]	內密	本月	ツウ	ゼンケン
ce	在…大使	我方	直ニ	明カ	乍ラ	テツ	通知
di	二月	在…代理大使	本日	タダシ	アン	十九日	會談
eg	來訪	本國政府	在…公使	ホレ	對案	豫メ	ナイ
em	本國	ラン	然ルベ(ク)	在…代理公使	會議	態度	アラザ(ル)
ew	ベク	豫テ	レイ	會計	在…總領事	ヤク	タキ
fo	ガン	ベン	考(フ)	レン	十八日	在…總領事代理 (事務代理)	ハツ
ge	承認	難(ク)	四月	カレ	聯合	ヘイ	在…領事
gu	會見	三月	ガツ	ベンボウ	發表	聯盟	然ルニ
hy	メン	極(メ)	主張	ゲキ	ベシ	カタ	八月
if	希臘	面談	ヘン	十七日	ゲン	ベツ	電信
in	移民	平和	面會	心得	クン	傳達	別電(第…號
ix	返電	イン	佛國	訓電	電送	主義	原因
mu	總理大臣	ノ如(ク)	否ヤ	ドク	見計(ヒ)	七月	シュク
no	例ヘバ	訓示	十六日	一方	ジツ	見込	試(ミ)
pi	訓令	同盟	總領事	情報	一般	英國	ミン
od	エイ	不取敢	條件	總督	ノミ	一般的	假令
oy	申添(フ)	條項	取扱(ヒ)	五月	ソツ	述ベ	委細
re	, comma	十五日	専ラ	取計(ヒ)	波蘭	國民	ニ依ル
sa	故	一 横線	波斯	モシ	國際	西比利亞	ステートメント
uc	從來	行懸	… 點線	コン	六月	取極(メ)	露國
uz	何分	ゾン	コンミット	/ 斜線	太平洋	若ハ	取消(シ)
wu	十四日	困難	ゼンゴ	行惱(ミ)	% パーセント	増加	求(メ)
xy	根本	前段	ナン	ゾウ	ユウ	? 疑問點	歐米

on both occasions Friedman's cryptological evidence was sufficiently damning to convict the conspirators. At the San Francisco trial, one of the defendants, who had managed to smuggle a revolver into the courtroom, shot and killed a compatriot who was testifying for the government. The assassin was then killed by a marshall shooting over the crowd.

Friedman's work began to attract attention. The British, who had been spared an insurrection thanks largely to Friedman, sent him some test messages enciphered by a new device they were considering adopting for use in the British Army. They were so pleased with the machine that some of them feared to introduce it lest the Germans capture it and use it themselves. With some adaptations by the enemy, they thought, it might produce ciphers that they themselves would be unable to crack.

William and Elizebeth Friedman went to work on the five enciphered messages. Within three hours of receiving them Friedman cabled their plaintexts back to London. The first message read, ironically, "This cipher is absolutely undecipherable." That spelled the end of the new cipher machine's usefulness.

Shortly after the war, the Friedmans left Riverbank, which was still concerned with the endless Bacon-Shakespeare controversy, and Friedman began his career with the Signal Corps. For the next 10 years he perfected his skills both as a cryptographer and as a cryptanalyst. He also wrote a major work on the subject, entitled *Elements of Cryptanalysis* (a word he coined himself).

Friedman's Signal Intelligence Service began operating in 1930. The following year saw the beginning of Japan's march of conquest through Asia. The Japanese invaded China, and in the following years continued to wage war in that vast country, meeting steady resistance from the Chinese. They began building up their navy, in defiance of the disarmament treaties. They also started a campaign of harassment of the United States, molesting American hospitals and missions in China and sinking an American gunboat. To cloak all these aggressive plans they devised several extremely complex codes and ciphers. The most complex of them all—the one used for the most secret communications—was known to the American code-breakers as PURPLE.

Cipher Machines

The name PURPLE traced its origins to the custom in American military circles of referring to Japan by the codeword ORANGE. The first formidable code put into service by the Japanese was dubbed RED; and so the even more complex cipher that appeared in the late 1930s was named according to the color progression established by the two previous codewords. PURPLE was a machine cipher, and the machine that produced it was called by the Japanese "97-shiki O-bun In-ji-ki."

Translated, the name is Alphabetical Typewriter 2597, that being the year of its introduction in the Japanese calendar (1937 according to the Western calendar).

By that time, Friedman's SIS had grown considerably. It also had an "opposite number" in the navy, known as OP-20-G, which shared with the SIS the task of deciphering the increasing flood of Japanese intercepts. But PURPLE was in a class by itself. Breaking its secrets was to give the SIS 20 months' grueling labor and Friedman himself a nervous breakdown.

The Japanese Foreign Office was completely convinced of the impregnability of its cipher machine. Even after a few notable lapses of security in America that showed the Japanese the possibility of their codes being broken, the Foreign Office merely made the token gesture of having "State Secret" painted in red letters on each PURPLE machine.

The machine resembled the ENIGMA cipher machine used by the Germans during World War II, whose cipher was also cracked by the Allies. It converted a plaintext message into cipher text by leading the original letters of the plaintext through an extremely complex maze (see diagram on page 70). The operator of the PURPLE machine would type a letter of the plaintext on the first typewriter in the system. An electric impulse ran from each letter through a wire ending in a plug, which had been inserted into a kind of pegboard in a prearranged pattern. The impulse ran through the pegboard into the rotor machine

Above: a Japanese telecommunications room in occupied China. Here they gathered information on the movements of the American and British navies throughout the Far East.

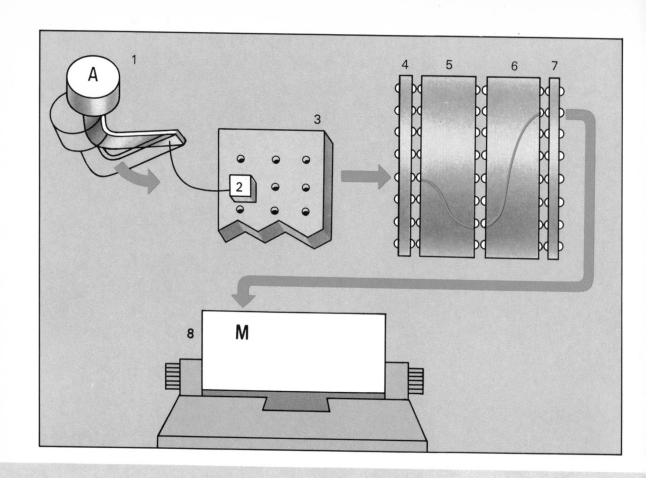

itself and emerged as a typewritten cipher text via the second typewriter. With a PURPLE machine both enciphering and deciphering were routine processes.

Reconstructing the devious workings of this machine from intercepted enciphered messages was anything but routine. It was a laborious and often exasperating process of educated guessing—trying to match newspaper stories, diplomatic notes passed on from the State Department, and other available information with the latest intercepts to see if any pattern could be discerned. Eventually, the work paid off, and SIS was able to construct a machine that would duplicate the action of the original Japanese model. It was a makeshift-looking machine and occasionally it sparked and made aggressive whirring noises. But it did the job.

The U.S. Navy Intelligence also acquired a machine, and after that the two cryptanalytic bureaus supplied the top military and government personnel with a stream of intercepts that went under the code-name MAGIC. On December 7, 1941 they were in fact better equipped for deciphering PURPLE messages than the Japanese embassy itself.

The two weeks preceding this "date which will live in infamy," as Roosevelt called it, had been full of ominous messages, both open and secret. On November 20, Ambassador Nomura had presented to Secretary of State Hull an ultimatum from his country demanding that the United States—among other things—acquiesce to further Japanese conquests in Asia and supply Japan with the oil she required (the United States having previously stopped this supply). The ambassador had been instructed by his government that it was important to obtain American agreement to these terms by November 29: "After that things are automatically going to happen."

On November 26, the two main Japanese carrier divisions started moving silently south toward their target, while Japanese-American negotiations continued. A day later, the Americans eavesdropped on a Tokyo-Washington telephone conversation that seemed to be about family matters. A "Miss Kimiko" and a "Miss Fumeko" figured in this apparently casual gossip. There was a "matrimonial question," which the Japanese ambassador was urged to pursue. He in turn inquired of his friend at the Foreign Office, "Does it seem as if a child might be born?" The answer was affirmative.

It was not too difficult for the Americans to deduce from the context of these remarks that "Miss Kimiko" and "Miss Fumeko" represented President Roosevelt and Secretary of State Hull respectively and that the "matrimonial question" referred to the negotiations. As for the "birth of the child," this was probably a crisis of some kind, an attack perhaps; but where would the "birth" take place?

For the next few days the air and the telegraph lines were full of coded Japanese messages, which kept the U.S. cryptanalysts fully occupied. Some 100 feet of teletype paper came into the offices each day for translation. Most of the information was useless—apparently an attempt on the part of the Japanese to confuse their adversaries. The really vital information—the location and direction of the Japanese carrier divisions—remained hidden. On December 1, Lieutenant Commander Joseph Rochefort, the director of intelligence for the 14th Naval District in Pearl Harbor, admitted to Admiral Kimmel, "I do not know where they are," but said he thought they were in home waters (that is, near Japan).

On December 1 an exchange between Germany and Japan was translated and conveyed to Roosevelt. The German Foreign Minister was reported as saying, "Should Japan become engaged in a war against the United States, Germany, of course, would join the war immediately." And the Japanese reply was ". . . there is extreme danger that war may suddenly break out between the Anglo-Saxon nations and Japan through some clash of arms and . . . the time of the breaking out of this war may come quicker than anyone dreams."

On the same day a message in the PURPLE cipher from Tokyo to its Washington embassy seemed to imply that the United States might not be the target. It concerned the destruction of code and cipher machines—a sign of imminent hostilities. "The four offices in London, Hong Kong, Singapore, and Manilla have been instructed to abandon the use of the code machines and to dispose of them. The machine in Batavia [Djakarta] has been returned to Japan. . . . the U.S. (office) retains the machines and the machine codes." It seemed possible that the attack would be on one of the British or Dutch possessions, which would give the United States a little more time to build up her military strength.

Yet only two days later, December 3, anyone passing the Japanese embassy on Massachusetts Avenue might have seen smoke rising from behind the embassy's walled garden. The Japanese had received instructions to burn their code books. And within the embassy the code clerks, armed with screwdrivers and hammers, were dismantling and beating to twisted fragments one of their precious cipher machines. The job completed, they sent back to Tokyo the single codeword HARUNA, to say that all was ready. They now had one operational machine left—a fact that was to prove of some importance.

On the evening of December 6, President Roosevelt decided to send a personal appeal for peace to Emperor Hirohito. It included the words: "I address myself to Your Majesty at this moment in the fervent hope that Your Majesty may, as I am doing, give thought in this definite emergency to ways of dispelling the dark clouds."

The president's message took only an hour to be sent, via telegraph, to Tokyo. Whether or not the message would have had any effect is impossible to guess. It did not reach its destination in time. Had it gone out in plain English it would have arrived at the emperor's palace shortly after its arrival in

Below: Secretary of State Cordell Hull with Japan's ambassador Nomura (left) and the special envoy Kurusu on their way to the White House for peace negotiations a week before the Japanese attack.

Tokyo. It would also have arrived promptly had it gone out in top security code. Instead, it went out in "gray" code—an everyday code selected for speed and simplicity of transmission. As a result, it got stuck in a log jam of other messages. A censor in Tokyo was simply carrying out orders to hold up all trans-oceanic traffic for five hours one day and 10 hours the next. The president's message took 10 hours to reach the American embassy. By that time, Admiral Nagumo's fleet was within two hours of its target.

Before the president's message had even been sent, the Japanese cryptographers had enciphered and released the first 13 parts of their message to the United States government and passed them to the Central Telegraph Office for transmission. The message was also sent via radio. The last part of the message, which contained the actual breaking off of negotiations, was held back for security reasons and would be released at the last possible moment. The Japanese embassy was instructed to prepare a presentable copy of the message and await instructions regarding its delivery.

As the separate parts of the message came over the radio, the naval radio station in Bainbridge Island, near Seattle, picked them up and sent them by teletype to Washington. There, the cryptanalysts of OP-20-G ran some of the parts through their PURPLE machine, sending others to their opposite numbers in SIS, who—though officially off duty that afternoon—had come back to the office when word was received that the long-awaited reply to Hull's latest proposals would be coming in.

By 8:45 that Saturday evening, the first 13 parts of the message

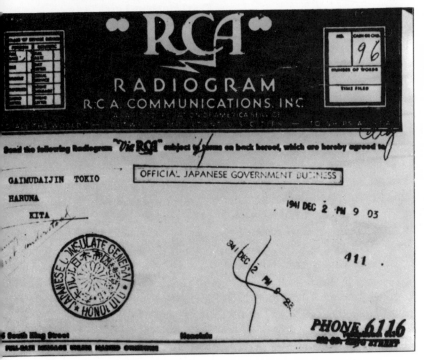

Left: this telegram bearing the single codeword HARUNA was sent by the embassy in Washington to inform the Japanese government that the codes had been destroyed.

73

had been received and deciphered. Several typed copies of this latest batch of MAGIC were in folders awaiting delivery to the usual recipients. They were distributed by Lieutenant Alwin Kramer, head of the translation section of OP-20-G.

President Roosevelt read his copy of the message and said to his friend Harry Hopkins, who was with him, "This means war."

Meanwhile, both the code clerks in the Japanese embassy and the code-breakers of OP-20-G and SIS were anxiously awaiting the final 14th part of the message. When Kramer arrived at his office at 7:30 the following morning he saw that the final part had arrived and been decoded and translated by his staff. He had copies prepared, and delivered some of them himself. When he returned to his office he found that another PURPLE message had come in. This one read as follows:

"Will the Ambassador please submit to the United States government (if possible to the Secretary of State) our reply to the United States at 1:00 p.m. on the 7th, your time." In addition, there was a message instructing the embassy not to use an ordinary clerk in preparing the message for presentation and another message ordering the destruction of the remaining PURPLE machine.

The peculiar timing of the message—midday on a Sunday—immediately struck Kramer as significant. He quickly figured that the hour of the deadline would be early morning in Hawaii and about two hours before dawn in Malaya, an area the Japanese had been threatening with ships and troops. It seemed clear that the 1:00 p.m. delivery of the Japanese message was meant to precede, very slightly, an early morning attack somewhere in the Pacific.

It was then shortly after 10:30 a.m. Only two and a half hours remained before the official delivery of the message by the Japanese and perhaps not much more time before an attack. Aware of the urgency of his mission Kramer hurried through the streets of Washington, delivering the MAGIC to the Navy Department, the State Department, and the War Department. By 11:30, Admiral Stark, Secretary of State Hull, and General Marshall had received the 1:00 p.m. message, and soon afterward Marshall, after conferring with Stark, sent his warning to Pearl Harbor.

Meanwhile the Japanese embassy code clerks were decoding the morning's messages, with no particular sense of urgency. The first secretary, Okumura, was typing up the first 13 parts of the ultimatum. Then one of the clerks put a newly arrived message through the PURPLE machine and found that it directed the embassy to deliver the *complete* ultimatum by 1:00 p.m. Where was part 14?

Then there began a frantic search through the incoming cables for the missing part. With only one PURPLE machine left for deciphering, the clerks were at a disadvantage. Moreover, Okumura was having troubles with his typing. Several inser-

Right: Rear Admiral H. R. Stark, Chief of Naval Operations, addressing the Appropriations Committee of the House of Representatives in 1940 on the need to build up the U.S. Navy. Stark and Chief of Staff George C. Marshall made the decision to warn Pearl Harbor—too late—of a possible attack.

Right: a drawing from the film *Tora Tora* ("Tiger Tiger") showing Japanese planes taking off from the aircraft carriers for the strike on Pearl Harbor. Later, Admiral Yamamoto, who had planned the attack, observed: "I fear that we have only awakened a sleeping giant, and his reaction will be terrible."

tions had been sent up to him by the code clerks, which meant retyping several pages. Finally, the 14th part was found and deciphered. Still, Okumura labored at his machine. A stickler for form, he felt he could not submit a declaration of war against the United States that was a mass of typing errors and re-translations. Again and again he tore the paper out of his machine and started a page afresh. Ambassador Nomura hovered at his elbow in a state of agitation. As the 1:00 p.m. deadline passed, the embassy phoned Secretary of State Hull and asked that the appointment with him that they had requested earlier should be postponed for an hour.

Finally, at 1:50 p.m., 25 minutes after the Japanese *blitzkrieg* had begun over Pearl Harbor, Okumura finished his work. Fifteen minutes later, as Nomura and Kurusu sat in the State Department waiting to see Hull, Roosevelt phoned Hull to pass on the unconfirmed report that Pearl Harbor had been attacked. The Japanese then delivered their message to Hull, unaware as they faced the angry Secretary of State that the warlords of their nation were at that moment destroying the American Pacific Fleet.

A full inquiry into the disaster of Pearl Harbor revealed a number of errors of judgment on the part of the American military and political leaders. But the cryptanalytic bureaus emerged very creditably from the investigation. Their speed in presenting decipherments from the formidable PURPLE

Above: Douglas Dauntless dive bombers in the Battle of Midway. Waves of these planes, taking off from American aircraft carriers, destroyed most of the Japanese ships lost during this decisive battle.

Above right: a Japanese heavy cruiser on fire after being attacked by U.S. aircraft at Midway. This was the first naval battle in which the two opposing naval forces never actually came into contact, the action consisting of attacks on the ships by carrier-launched aircraft.

machine—in advance of the Japanese, its rightful possessors—remains one of the most remarkable feats in cryptanalytic history. And in the course of the war that followed, the code-breakers were in a position to help their country several times to gain its revenge against the aggressor.

The Mystery of AF

One such incident took place near a group of tiny islands called Midway, some 1200 miles northeast of Hawaii. The battle fought here was to be the turning point of the war in the Pacific and one of the most decisive battles in history. It was also an event of the highest drama for America's code-breakers. For two days in June 1942, the fate of the U.S. Fleet (rebuilt since Pearl Harbor) hung on the meaning of two letters: AF.

Between December 1941 and June 1942, the Japanese Navy under the command of Admiral Yamamoto had swept from one victory to another. Indeed, the Japanese themselves would later admit that at the time they were suffering from "Victory disease," the feeling that nothing on land or sea could stop their triumphal progress. Yamamoto knew how essential it was to achieve victories in rapid succession. Given time, America could starve Japan of fuel. So America must not be given time. At Midway he would deal the U.S. Fleet a crushing defeat that would put it permanently out of action.

Below: Admiral C. W. Nimitz (right), Commander in Chief of the Pacific Fleet, on an inspection tour of Midway. He called the Battle of Midway "a victory of intelligence."

Part of his strategy was to stage a diversionary attack on the Aleutian Islands. This would lure part of the U.S. Fleet away from the main conflict. For the attack to be successful, it was of course vital that the Americans not know that Midway was to be the target.

On May 20, 1942 Yamamoto broadcast his plans for the final destruction of the U.S. Fleet in a lengthy series of orders to his own fleet. And on the same day, in a well-guarded cellar in Pearl Harbor, the U.S. Navy's Combat Intelligence Unit, under the direction of Rochefort, started to break into the stream of five-digit codegroups that concealed the admiral's intentions.

Their task was the breaking of the Japanese naval code JN 25, which consisted of 45,000 codegroups that were then enciphered by a further 50,000 groups. For months the Intelligence Unit had been laboring to crack this code, working shifts of 12 hours on the job and 12 hours off. Assisting them in their work were IBM tabulators. The age of machine cryptanalysis had arrived. As the code-breakers deduced or stumbled onto the meaning of codegroups, they put them through the IBM apparatus so that they were recorded on punched cards. By early May, the cryptanalysts could read about 90 percent of a typical JN 25 cryptogram.

Yamamoto's long and detailed instructions to his navy presented somewhat more of a challenge. Throughout the last week of May the unit struggled with the text, until finally the picture of the projected battle emerged. But it was not a complete picture. The where and when of the intended operation remained hidden in mysterious letter groups that defied analysis.

The key location was AF. Already, the cryptanalysts suspected that AF meant Midway. Two Japanese planes had mentioned AF while flying in that region and their exchange had been picked up by the American listening posts. But the Commander of the U.S. Fleet, Admiral Nimitz, hesitated to concentrate his entire force there on such a vague hypothesis.

Rochefort then employed one of the oldest tricks of the game. He arranged for the U.S. garrison on Midway to broadcast the news that they were short of fresh water, using a code that Rochefort knew the Japanese had broken. This would be an interesting piece of information for the listening Japanese.

For two days the Americans waited for the fish to bite on the bait. And then they were rewarded: Yamamoto broadcast to his fleet, "AF is short of fresh water."

By this time, the unit had managed to determine the probable date of the attack, and Nimitz was able to get his fleet to Midway and surprise the enemy. The Americans destroyed all four of the big Japanese aircraft carriers that had launched the Pearl Harbor attack. Admiral Nagumo, who had commanded that attack as well as this one, was on the carrier *Agaki*. The American "Hell Divers" plunged down upon his ship and dropped their load of 1000-pound bombs. One of these ripped into the depths of the carrier, exploding its torpedoes and setting them off in an explosion that raised the flight deck into a dome of torn and blistered metal. The *Agaki*'s planes were thrown about like toys.

By the end of the battle, the Japanese Navy was so crippled that it would not be able to recover fully for the duration of the war.

The code-breakers, with their pencils and paper and their IBM machines, were about 1000 miles from the carnage at Midway. But without their work Midway would not have taken the course it did. As Admiral Nimitz later observed: "Midway was essentially a victory of intelligence."

The Death of Admiral Yamamoto

Yamamoto's carefully planned surprise attack had backfired, largely due to the skill of America's code-breakers. Nearly a year later, he himself was to fall victim to their skill.

In the spring of 1943 things were going badly for the Japanese. They had been pushed off many of their Pacific island strongholds, and now the Allies were about to complete their conquest of the Solomon Islands with an attack on the important Japanese base in Rabaul. But the Japanese were continuing, with some success, to send air attacks against the Allies, and in the spring Yamamoto came to Rabaul to direct operations personally. On April 13, his headquarters broadcast to the various bases in the Solomons the news that on April 18 Yamamoto would make a tour of inspection. The message included all the details of his timetable and type of aircraft, and of the protective aircraft that would accompany him.

This interesting message was picked up and deciphered by FRUPAC (Fleet Radio Unit, Pacific Fleet), as the Hawaii-based cryptanalytic unit was now called. Here was a tempting opportunity. Yamamoto was the ablest naval commander the Japanese had. His death would mean replacement by someone almost certainly inferior to him as a strategist and leader. It would also demoralize the Japanese.

A passionate debate began among the top brass in Washington. Even in the context of a savagely fought war, was there not something underhand in a deliberate assassination? And what of the security angle: might not the Japanese guess—and then rectify—the breach in their code security?

The latter question was quickly dismissed; conceivably, some friendly natives might have slipped news of Yamamoto's visit to the Americans. And whether or not killing Yamamoto was immoral, it would be a major psychological defeat for the enemy. The plan received the go-ahead.

At 6:00 a.m. on the morning of April 18, exactly on schedule as always and dressed in full formal rig including a ceremonial samurai sword, Admiral Isoroku Yamamoto left Rabaul on the first leg of his tour. His plane was to touch down in Ballale, on the island of Bougainville, at 8:00 a.m.

Exactly 35 minutes earlier, 18 American Lightning planes

Above: Admiral Isoroku Yamamoto, Commander in Chief of Japan's Combined Fleet until his death in 1943 when his plane was shot down by Army Air Force fighters. The planes knew where and when to strike through the work of Allied cryptanalysts in decoding Japanese messages.

had taken off from Guadalcanal Island, some 700 miles to the south of Bougainville, to rendezvous with the admiral. They flew low over the water to avoid detection by Japanese radar. The man in charge of the mission, Captain Thomas Lanphier of the U.S. Army Air Force, had been skeptical of its chance of success. The ocean is vast, and the chance of back room intelligence experts accurately predicting the precise position of a handful of planes at a precise time in all that vastness seemed remote.

And yet the intelligence men were right. There in the gun sights was a pack of Japanese planes in exactly the predicted position. While 14 of the Lightnings engaged Yamamoto's escort fighters, Lanphier pursued the bomber in which the Admiral himself was flying.

"I fired a long steady burst across the bomber's course of flight from approximately right angles. The bomber's right engine, then its right wing, burst into flame. . . . As I moved into range of Yamamoto's bomber and its cannon, the bomber's wing tore off. The bomber plunged into the jungle."

Lanphier and all but one of the other members of the mission returned safely to their base. Later, Yamamoto's body was found still in its seat, with its chin on the samurai sword. It was carefully extricated from the ruins of the plane and cremated. The Japanese mourned him deeply, and his successor observed simply, "There was only one Yamamoto, and no one is able to replace him."

Below: the decaying wreckage of the Mitsubishi bomber in the jungle of Bougainville Island where it was shot down more than 30 years ago. The body of its distinguished passenger Admiral Yamamoto was discovered inside it, leaning on his samurai sword.

World War II: ULTRA

5

Above: *Battle of Britain,* a graphic depiction of Britain's heroic defense against the all-out German air onslaught from August to mid-September 1940 by war artist Paul Nash. The sky is a jumble of condensation trails made by RAF fighters as they attack enemy bombers. In the lower left-hand corner can be seen balloons intended as protection against dive bombing. It was not known until many years after the war's end that the winning strategy of the battle owed much to the cracking of German codes by British cryptanalysts. Their access to confidential Nazi information was called ULTRA. **Left:** a wartime photograph of German military staff surveying the English coast across the Straits of Dover from France, taken on July 1, 1940. At right (arrowed) is Hermann Goering, chief of the German Air Force.

In the annals of World War II the Battle of Britain stands out as one of the hardest fought and most decisive encounters. Yet for 35 years after the war it was surrounded by mystery.

For Reich Marshal Hermann Goering, the Nazi commander who lost the battle, Britain's tactics in the skies of southern England in the late summer of 1940 were baffling. For Air Marshal Hugh Caswall Dowding, chief of Britain's Fighter Command, the attempt to baffle was deliberate. How did Dowding win with some 1200 planes against three times that number? And why, in spite of his success against such odds, was he stripped of his command? The answer to both these questions lies in the ULTRA secret, a secret of such dimensions that only the word "ultra" seemed sufficient to describe it.

To understand how ULTRA both helped and hurt Dowding, a quick look at the Battle of Britain is important. The Nazi air attack on Britain in 1940 was intended to destroy the Royal Air Force in order to leave the way clear for an invasion by sea. It had to be in the summer to take advantage of the weather, and it had to be brief so that there would be time to give 10 days' notice to the occupying forces. The last available day when wind and tide would favor a Channel crossing was September 27. Goering was confident he could crush the RAF by September 17 to meet the deadline for the invasion alert. On August 8 he dispatched the message his airmen had been waiting for.

"From Reich Marshal Goering to all units of Luftwaffe 2, 3, and 5. Operation Eagle. Within a short period you will wipe the British Air Force from the sky. Heil Hitler."

However, things did not go that way. Day by day that August and early September the German planes attacked. Day by day Dowding and his closest associate, Air Vice Marshal Park, sent up only a few planes against superior odds. The losses, heavy on both sides, were exaggerated by propaganda. But the few precious RAF squadrons flew on, partly because by sparing use the pilots could rest and the equipment could be repaired before the next onslaught.

The fact that Dowding held back on the number of planes in the air at any one time became the point of criticism. Why, his critics asked, did he insist on husbanding his resources so

sparingly. Why did he keep so many eager pilots on the ground? As the summer wore on, those who argued for a bigger show of force grew more clamorous.

Dowding finally allowed his men to strike with all they had on September 15. The result seemed only to prove his critics' point. That day, 250 German bombers, supported by 700 fighters, crossed the Channel. They were met by more British planes than the Germans knew existed. Eleven squadrons were flung in over London, six more over nearby Rochester, Kent. Astounded, the Germans scurried for home—only to meet a further four squadrons to harry them to the coast. It was only two days before the very last day of the year on which an invasion plan could be safely announced. Goering decided on September 15. In one final spasm of determination, he turned the bombers around for a second attack. He could not believe that the British had anyone left in the air.

Unbelievably, 19 squadrons and part of a 20th were up in the air to do battle all over again. In the debacle of the second attack of the day, many more German planes were lost. The survivors turned and fled. The last chance of securing a victory in the air was gone forever, and the land base for the invasion of Normandy was secured.

Among those who fought that September day were the men of Britain's Number 12 Group, under the command of Air Vice Marshal Leigh-Mallory. Leigh-Mallory had brought three

Above: Air Marshal Hugh Caswall Dowding, head of Britain's Fighter Command during the Battle of Britain. Though with the aid of secret ULTRA information Dowding won the battle, he was later removed from his command. He never revealed the source of his all-important information.

**Above: a British Spitfire—
fast and maneuverable—attacks
a ponderous German bomber in
war-torn skies over Britain.**

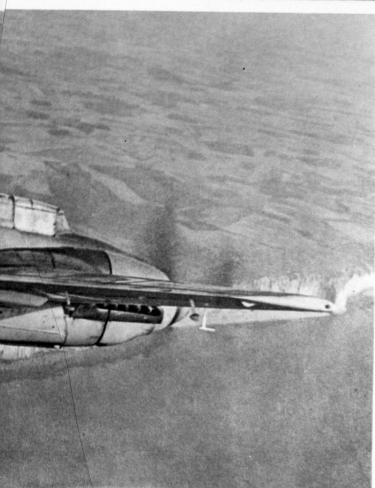

**Left: a Messerschmitt 110 over
the cliffs of southeast England.
These German fighter escort
planes helped smash the poorly
equipped Polish and French air
forces in earlier battles, but
suffered heavily against British Spitfires and Hurricanes.**

squadrons of Hurricanes and two of Spitfires south of the ames to join in the fracas. But Dowding reprimanded him, ause by Dowding's rule book he should have stayed out of encounter. This made Leigh-Mallory join Dowding's tics. "Look what happened," they said, "when we did throw all we had: we won."

In the October after the battle, Dowding was summo to face his critics at a bitter encounter at the Air Ministr He looked tired and older. Against a barrage of criticism nd questioning he stayed silent. By the year's end he had en removed from his command and sent on the humble m on of selling an airplane engine to the United States. A year er he was shuffled onto the retired list. When the Air Mi ry produced a pamphlet on the famous Battle of Britain, Dowd's name was not even mentioned. Yet Dowding—whose of l biography quotes his reputation as a "hard man, stubb, merciless"—accepted his humiliation with quiet good gr. "I remain under no sense of grievance," he said. "The Germ lost the battle and that was what really mattered."

Why didn't Dowding defend himself and save his posit and reputation? At the time only Dowding, Prime Minis Winston Churchill himself, and a handful of men and wom

Below: a squadron of British Hurricanes, backbone of Fighter Command. This plane was extremely sturdy, capable of taking great punishment, but Britain had far too few of them for total defense. That is why Dowding, armed with secret information about German attack plans, used them sparingly, in the face of critics.

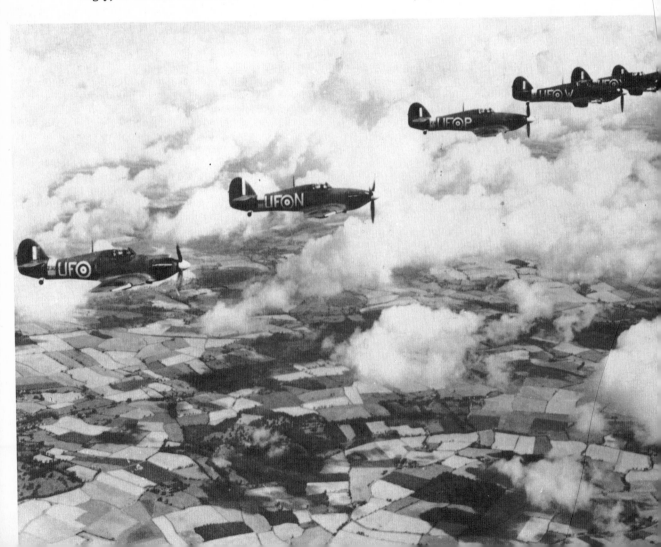

in the world knew precisely why the Battle of Britain had been fought Dowding's way.

Dowding was not at liberty to use the only defense he had. He could not explain that at all times—before the battle, during the battle and after the battle—he was privy to the inmost thoughts and plans of Goering. He could not reveal that through possession of the ULTRA secret—the day-by-day interception of Germany's most secure code—the British knew the whole strategy of the Luftwaffe. He could not say that he sent so few planes up because he and Churchill knew that the Luftwaffe's hope was to draw all the planes into the air.

Why was the RAF finally flung wholeheartedly into combat on September 15? Because Dowding knew this was Goering's last fling. But he would not tell how he knew. Why were the British still in the air to meet them on the second wave of the attack? Because Dowding knew, within minutes of the order being given, of Goering's desperate determination to throw the Luftwaffe back into the fray. But he failed to explain himself because he was loyal to his pledge of secrecy about ULTRA.

Dowding was asked to make one of the most difficult sacrifices of all: to protect the ULTRA secret by the acceptance of personal disgrace. It was a secret worth keeping, however. In

Below: a painting by Walter Bayes shows two Germans parachuting from their destroyed plane over Buckingham Palace. Hitler's decision to bomb London intensively was a strategic mistake because it left the airfields temporarily free from attack, and this gave the hard-pressed fighter pilots a needed, if brief, respite.

"LET US GO FORWARD TOGETHER"

every major campaign of the war, ULTRA enabled the Allies to listen in on the most private communications of the Nazi leaders. It was a source of information that remained available to the end—to the last, half-deranged ramblings of Hitler in his doomed Berlin bunker.

Churchill, who referred to ULTRA in private as "my most secret source," was as much bound by secrecy as anyone else in the know. Throughout his monumental history of the war, no mention appears of the role that was played by codes in the attainment of the final victory.

In the years after the war's end, some possessors of the secret pleaded from time to time, and in the highest circles, for permission to speak and set the record straight. But in Britain those involved in any secret undertakings of the government are bound by a rule to keep silence for 30 years. So they were refused permission to speak. Besides, the effect of some of the decisions made by those operating out of knowledge of the German intentions had wide implications, even for us today.

The dilemma of what to do with the secret information obtained through their work is a real one for the code-breakers. If they take evasive action, they risk alerting the enemy that their movements are known. If they do not act on their information, the lives of their own people may be lost. Some historians have suggested that Churchill was faced with just such a decision

Above left: a poster issued by the Ministry of Information after Winston Churchill became prime minister in May 1940. Churchill made some of his most important and far-reaching decisions on the basis of secret ULTRA information.

Above: the city of Coventry in ruins after the German air raids of 1940. It has been said that Churchill had prior knowledge by means of ULTRA of a heavy German attack on one of a number of English cities, including Coventry, but that he could not act on this information because, by such action, he would have given away to the Germans that he was using what he called his "most secret source". In any event, there was little that even Churchill could have done to prevent the tragic destruction and loss of life in the raids on Coventry.

Right: war artist Laura Knight depicts the defensive balloon barrage set up around Coventry.

involving ULTRA. Through his "most secret source," they suggest, he had prior warning that the Germans were planning heavy raids on a number of English cities in November 1940. One writer has even asserted that Churchill had 48 hours warning that Coventry was to be the target of the raid that in fact took place on November 14, 1940. If he is correct in his assertion, then the decision to ignore the warning was indeed a difficult one.

Enigma Machines

From the point of view of British intelligence, the ULTRA story began on a day in 1938 when a young Pole revealed the activities of a highly secret East German factory. He had been employed there, but was dismissed by the Germans for security reasons. No friend to the German cause, he had taken careful notice of the machines that were in full production in the factory. They were called "Enigma" machines.

That Germany was preparing to fight a war with a cipher machine was in itself no surprise. The Americans, Italians, Japanese, and others were busy in the prewar years perfecting the device that was to move to the forefront of the cryptographers' armory. For the new-style warfare—fast moving, complex, and widely distributed—cumbersome code books were as outdated as the cavalry. As for one-time pads—the unbreakable code—the entire printing capacity of a nation would have been needed to produce the volume of pads required.

In the illustration: *W.R.N.S. Cypher Office Naval C-in-C's H.Q. June 1944*

Above: the cipher room of the Women's Royal Naval Service in 1944, painted by Barnett Freedman. The navy persisted in the use of its traditional codes, with the result that the Nazis broke them all before the war had even started. This led to a disastrous loss of shipping.

Between World Wars I and II no less than four inventors had come up independently with the right answer: a compact machine that transferred clear text into the most incomprehensible code. Only one of the four lived to prosper from his inventiveness.

The advantage of cipher machines can be seen more clearly by looking at an organization that spurned them: the British Navy. Although cipher machines were introduced in the mid-1930s, the navy reported them as unreliable, unworkable in bad weather, and far too complicated. Lord Mountbatten, later Admiral of the Fleet and then an enthusiast for the cipher machine, was blunt on the reason for the failure of the machines. He claimed the experiment had been sabotaged. The navy, conservative by nature, stayed with its traditional codes during World War II. When the United States joined the war, American commanders were horrified to discover how "slow, old-fashioned, and dangerous" the naval ciphers were. In fact, Germany's code-breakers had cracked them before the war even started. In the first four years of the conflict, the Germans destroyed 11.5 million tons of British shipping in the North Atlantic.

In a global war, the capture of just one ship and its code books could require the urgent distribution of thousands of new codes across hazardous seas. Cipher machines avoided this problem.

The general principle of the new electrical machines—of

which the German Enigma device was an example—was rotary disks, half an inch thick and up to four inches in diameter, and made of insulating material. On each side of each disk are 26 electrical contacts in the form of metal studs. Each stud on one side of a disk is joined to one on the other side of the same disk by a wire. The wire does not run to the immediate opposite contact, however, but at random. In other words, if a contact on one side of the disk stands for the letter A, the wire connecting it to the other side would connect not with the contact in the A position, but with that in some other position. In a cipher machine, up to six disks are mounted between two fixed plates, each of which is also studded with a ring of 26 contacts. The diagram on page 70 shows a profile view of the studded disks and their wiring.

A typist strikes the letter A and a current passes through the fixed contact designating A on the first of the plates between which the disks are sandwiched. It then passes to the contact on the first disk, through that disk and out at another point to the contact on the second disk, and so on. At the end of its mazelike path, the current emerges at the second fixed plate and indicates the enciphered letter by a lamp bulb or by a print-out.

If the disks were immovable, an alphabet could be changed into only one other alphabet. But if, after each letter is enciphered, one or more of the rotors moves a step, a new alphabet can be created. The disks of a cipher machine rotate, and the immense number of alphabets so created is the strength of the device. Cryptanalysts look for repetitions, for the clues that will show up a key word or a key letter. But in a three-rotor machine the number of possible positions for all three disks in relation to the fixed plates is $26 \times 26 \times 26$. On a five-rotor machine it is $26 \times 26 \times 26 \times 26 \times 26$—a staggering 11,881,376 different alphabets to go through before the encoder starts repeating himself and the cryptanalyst discovers the repetition.

The Enigma machine was impressive enough to convince Hitler that it was what he required to back up his military blitzkrieg with a totally secure code system. For the inventor of the Enigma machine, Arthur Scherbius, Hitler's decision came too late.

Scherbius had struggled hard to market his device in the 1920s. The company he launched in 1923 survived 11 years before its dissolution, and never paid a dividend. Scherbius went bankrupt and died before German production of his machine started.

Two other inventors of cipher machines suffered the same disappointment. In the United States, Edward Hugh Herbern spent the 1920s treading the same path as Scherbius. He invented a rotary machine, sank all his hopes for the future in it, formed a corporation, and went bankrupt. At the end of World War II Herbern filed a $50 million claim against the United States government. He said they had copied his machine and distributed it throughout the armed services. The case was

Above: the Enigma machine, a mechanical device for coding invented by the German Arthur Scherbius. Its keyboard is similar to a typewriter, but the letters strike rotary disks that choose substitute letters at random to create encoded messages.

89

settled with a payment of $30,000. But the embittered Herbern had died of old age, and the settlement was made on his estate.

These inventors arrived on the scene too soon. The inter-war world was not interested in devices that would help spies. That interest came when nations were at war. Only one of the four brilliant engineers who threw their creative energies into the development of the rotor machine was lucky. That was Boris Caesar Wilhelm Hagelin, a Swede who became a multimillionaire out of the cipher machine business.

Hagelin's first coup came in 1927. At that time he was already working in the cipher machine business—for Arvid Gerhard Damm, the third inventor of cipher machines. Damm's brain-

Right: Boris Hagelin, the man who made millions from the sale of a coding machine to the United States military. In 1940 he made a dangerous wartime journey from his native Sweden through Germany in order to get the machine to the United States before all travel ended. He is shown with a standard model below which is a message coded by the machine.

child was in financial trouble. Hearing that the Swedish Army was planning to buy the Scherbius Enigma machine, Hagelin swiftly made a few improvements of his own on the model of his employer, and won the order.

The unfortunate Damm died almost immediately thereafter, and Hagelin was well placed to buy the firm and fill the Swedish order. By the outbreak of war and the arrival of a world crowded with potential customers for a good cipher machine, Hagelin had headed for the United States. He only just made it.

Carrying a briefcase stuffed with blueprints and a bag full of dismantled cipher machine parts, Hagelin and his young wife sped by train from Stockholm to Italy as Europe fell around them to the Nazis. From Genoa he caught one of the last westward-bound ships of the war. The effort was worth it. His machine, known in the United States as Converter M209, became the choice for communication from top to bottom level. With a royalty on each of the 140,000 Hagelin machines produced for the United States armed services, he made millions of dollars.

To go back to 1938 and the disclosure about the Enigma machine to the British by the young Pole. News of the Enigma factory got a swift response from British intelligence. The informant, discreetly removed from Warsaw to Paris, was set the task of assisting in the construction of a huge wooden mock-up of Hitler's cipher machine. Other Polish ex-employees with long memories of their work in the factory kept London informed. London kept news of the possible prize a close secret. When word came from Poland that an operational machine was ready, it was fitting that the man sent to obtain one surreptitiously was a veteran of World War I's famous black chamber, Room 40—the quietly spoken Alastair Denniston.

The Enigma looked simple. It was battery powered and only the size of a typewriter. Letters struck on a typewriter keyboard were started on their complex path through the drums, soon to be displayed on a panel of glow lamps, each signifying a letter.

The ULTRA secret lay in front of Denniston, but it was still a secret. The mathematical computations needed to determine how the machine worked were formidable.

As head of the British government's Codes and Ciphers School, Denniston set out to acquire the best mathematical brains in Britain for this task. In ones and twos a team came together, some leaving first-rate academic positions to work in secrecy and at full stretch on the problems of Enigma.

The war began. The Enigma machine and those striving to unravel it were safely hidden in a 19th-century mansion near the nondescript South Midlands town of Bletchley. In the various departments of the British Secret Service only a handful knew about Enigma. Included was Colonel Stewart Menzies, chief of the whole Secret Service. Also included was a certain Group Captain F. W. Winterbotham, whose contribution to ULTRA's effectiveness proved as decisive as that of solving the mathematical problems involved.

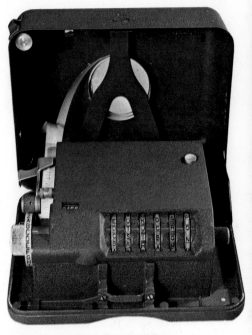

Above: the Hagelin machine, known in the United States as M209. With six rotor disks, it produces 101,405,850 different encoded letters before it begins to repeat itself—10 times more than a five-rotor machine.

Above: Bletchley Park, the big country mansion that was the headquarters of British crypt-analysts during World War II. It was here, in a temporary hut as seen on the left, that the brilliant work of decoding German secrets was carried out.

As the team started work, it was well aware that possession of the machine was the merest first step. After all, no one had expected that the machine would never be stolen, and the system for its security was not based on the idea that it would never fall into the wrong hands.

In the late 19th century, for example, one of the fathers of modern code-breaking, Jean Guillaume Hubert Victor François Alexandre Auguste Kerchkhoffs von Niewenhof, had stated what was to be a principle of military code usage. A good system, he declared, should not depend for secrecy on "code books, or whatever mechanical apparatus may be necessary." What had to remain secret was the *key*.

The rotor machine produces millions of alphabets, and the analyst has to work out not only the path taken through each rotor, but also the starting position of each rotor. This complex task is further complicated by the fact that the rotors fall into new arrangements at random.

The best starting point for learning how the system works is a piece of plaintext to compare with the enciphered text. Even if there are two messages that only begin with the same formal opening, it is a starting place.

Imagine, for example, that in the cipher text of a message the letter A appears twice in the first 26 letters of the message.

The analyst knows that this particular machine is designed with five rotors. He also knows that the rotors are geared, and that each one rotates until it has come full circle through 26 letter positions.

What, then, does the fact that the letter A appears twice in the course of 26 letters reveal? For a start, it indicates that through four of the five rotors, the paths taken by the electrical impulses must be the same. The analyst can "subtract" this effect from the problem in hand. Secondly, it is known how many spaces separate the first appearance of the letter A in the cryptogram from the second. Now the analyst knows that, whatever the letter being encoded on each occasion, the first rotor has moved that number of spaces between the two appearances. He or she still does not know what letter is being encoded, and cannot conclude that the letter A that emerges on the last rotor of the machine denotes an A position on the first rotor. But from this fragment of knowledge about the movement of the first rotor, progress can be made.

The analyst can see what happens at the 27th, 53rd, and 79th letters of the message because he knows that after every 26 letters the first rotor has completed a revolution and the second rotor has moved one place. Still without a clue to the meaning of the message, he can start to experiment with wiring up a machine in ways that will at least reproduce the message in hand.

Computers in Cryptanalysis

In so doing, the equations involved are monumental in quantity and length. Fortunately for the code-breakers, by 1940 a new invention of human genius—the computer—was born. To a computer, data in terms of millions of calculations are no obstacle. Even though the early computers were both unwieldy and unpredictable, they worked like magic. Winterbotham recalled his first sight of the device that was to defeat the Enigma machine. "Early in 1940 I was ushered with great solemnity into the shrine where stood a bronze-colored column surmounted by a larger circular bronze-colored face, like some Eastern Goddess who was destined to become the oracle of Bletchley, at least when she felt like it. She was an awesome piece of magic."

In February 1940, when the Germans started transmitting practice messages, the "piece of magic" read them!

The first messages took Bletchley six weeks of intensive effort to solve. Winterbotham was given the honor of presenting them in person to the Director of Air Intelligence, Charles Medhurst. Winterbotham showed Medhurst that the top-secret code of the German High Command was an open book to the British.

The Director's reaction astonished Winterbotham. He glanced at the messages and said politely: "You will have to do better than that."

Suddenly, Winterbotham realized how easily the hard-won

Above: Colonel Stewart Menzies, wartime chief of the British Secret Service. As befits a man involved in secret work, little is known of his career to this day. Even his autobiography was intended not for publication, but for record.

93

Above: a painting of the British evacuation of troops from Dunkirk in May–June 1940. The timing of the retreat was decided on the basis of ULTRA intelligence about Nazi strategy in the north of France.

secret could be revealed. The intelligence organization of the day were still fragmented; between the three armed services there was still misunderstanding and rivalry; between straightforward military men and espionage men there was still suspicion. Unless the ULTRA secret of the cracking of the Enigma machine code was properly guarded, it would not remain a secret for long. If ULTRA messages were passed out wholesale, and perhaps repeated on the airways in ciphers the Germans had already cracked, the Germans would soon find a new code, and all the advantage gained by the work at Bletchley would be lost.

Winterbotham had to devise a plan to protect ULTRA, and to hammer its importance into the heads of the highest in the land. There were two parts to the security system he proposed. First, it was suggested that there be only one official translation of ULTRA intelligence for all three services, to be made at Bletchley. Secondly, the services were not to pass on ULTRA

information at their own discretion and in their own codes. Instead, the ULTRA information was to go out on the unbreakable one-time pad system, and only to Special Liaison Units (SLU) in the field.

When Winterbotham took the plan to his chief, Colonel Menzies agreed to it. From a hut on the lawns of Bletchley Park, Winterbotham began to build a team that protected ULTRA throughout the rest of the war, and ensured that the enemies' secrets were placed speedily, accurately, and personally into the hands of top commanders in all theaters of the global conflict.

The first real information from ULTRA was awe-inspiring, but of only academic interest to the hard-pressed British military. In April 1940 the Enigma machines were busy relaying detailed information on the massive quantity of men and armor being wheeled into position for the Nazis' swift conquest of Belgium, the Netherlands, and France. It added up to an accurate picture of the German order of battle. Unfortunately, it was a battle that the British could in no way counteract at that time.

When the battle was unleashed in May 1940, the information pouring into Bletchley from the intercepted Enigma transmissions changed in style. Now the to-and-fro of real warfare was reflected in the messages—in particular, the German designs on the British Expeditionary Force (BEF), already in trouble on the mainland of Europe. If the BEF were destroyed, only the Channel would lie between the Germans and a successful invasion of Britain.

On April 23 General von Brauchitsch revealed what Germany had in mind for the BEF by an order to "continue the encircling movement with the utmost vigor." It was this ULTRA signal that convinced Churchill that it was time to pull the British forces back to the sea at all speed—and to muster the little boats off Dunkirk to rescue them when they got there. From then on Churchill took a personal interest in the ULTRA intelligence, and Group Captain Winterbotham had the task of taking more important messages directly to the Prime Minister. "With ULTRA in his hand, he now began to run the war himself, and did not cease to do so until the end of 1945," Winterbotham later recalled.

It became an oddly personal affair, this day-by-day listening in to the plans of the top Nazis. One expert in Bletchley's Hut 3, a prewar salesman, had made a special study of Hitler's speeches in the 1930s, and could translate his distinctive phraseology at a high speed. Goering's brutal style of wit became familiar to the code-breakers. All the time, the speed and reliability of decoding improved.

In July 1940, when Goering warned his generals of the planned invasion of Britain, Churchill was able to reply swiftly. His answer was not in code: it was the famous speech that told the world Britain would fight the Germans on the beaches and in the streets if necessary.

Above: General Erwin Rommel, commander of German forces in North Africa, photographed during the Libyan campaign. His defeat was hastened by the ability of the British to decode secret Nazi orders, often before Rommel himself got them.

The Battle of El Alamein

The Battle of Britain, the first major test of the ULTRA decoders, was but the first of a long series of successes. The team devoted to decoding grew in strength, and called for new giant computers. Its immediate task after the Battle of Britain had been won was to alert fire-fighting forces to air raids on London. But world-wide the role of ULTRA was just beginning. In 1941 the British learned of Hitler's plans in North Africa through ULTRA, including the appointment of General Erwin Rommel as commander.

In the desert war, both sides were well equipped with codes and with intelligence. The ULTRA team had four SLUs in the Middle East, serving the key generals directly in the way Winterbotham had ordered. But Rommel also had code intelligence of high quality. Through an Italian spy, Rommel had obtained the Americans' top-secret code. All the reports of Colonel Bonner Frank Fellers, the American military attaché in Cairo, were known immediately by the Nazi general. Fellers' reports were detailed and comprehensive. Within a few hours of being sent, his dispatches on the Allied situation in the desert were analyzed, translated, reenciphered, and on Rommel's table. Rommel's brilliant weaving and dodging that so baffled the British was much aided by his knowledge of British plans. When Fellers' dispatches were halted in mid-1942 on the British dis-

Left: British troops capturing the crew of a German tank at the height of the Battle of El Alamein. This German defeat in North Africa marked the point at which the tide of the war turned in favor of the Allies.

Below: a wartime portrait of Field Marshal Montgomery. He led the successful assault by British troops at El Alamein.

covery of their interception, Rommel began to falter. For Britain's 8th Army it was the chance to take the initiative again through ULTRA's aid.

Churchill, newly returned from Moscow, met Field Marshals Montgomery and Alexander in Egypt. They were able to study the complete intercepted text of Rommel's latest personal message to Hitler. It revealed his final plan to sweep his tanks northward and drive the 8th Army into the sea. The battle order was complete down to the date. Rommel, though stripped of coded intelligence, was making a last desperate effort to win.

When the attack came on August 31, 1942 Montgomery was waiting and well hidden. The Germans, used to reliance on coded intelligence, were not adept at the only alternative— aerial reconnaissance. On September 2, Rommel fell back, and could only await the onslaught of the counterattack. Again, the loss of Rommel's decoded intelligence kept him in the dark as to Montgomery's movements. On October 23, Montgomery opened up with 1000 cannon at El Alamein. Hitler ordered Rommel to stand firm to the last man. It was a style of order that the ULTRA cryptanalysts were to hear him make more than once before the war was over. It so happened that the British heard that command before Rommel himself: they had already decoded it when they picked up a perhaps disbelieving request to repeat it from Rommel's camp.

In a way, El Alamein was the beginning of the end of the war. "Before Alamein we never had a victory. After Alamein we never had a defeat," declared Churchill.

The United States and ULTRA

ULTRA analysts were on the offensive from then on. When the Americans entered the war Churchill personally briefed President Franklin Roosevelt on his "most secret source," and Winterbotham's list of those entitled to ULTRA information had to be enlarged. The responsibility of guarding its secrecy was heavier than ever. There was no shortage of people qualified to be put on the list, and likely to feel offended if refused. Winterbotham alone, however, could make an addition to that select rollcall—and he insisted that in any key war center, no more than five people should be in possession of the secrets of ULTRA.

Furthermore, only an SLU officer could communicate an ULTRA message to anyone on the list, and having handed over his transcript, it was his responsibility to retrieve and destroy it. No commander was permitted to refer to ULTRA in any order he made, nor to repeat any part of an ULTRA message. If any Allied action taken as a result of gaining ULTRA secrets seemed likely to alert the Germans that their signals had been intercepted, a cover operation was to be mounted to persuade the enemy that the information had been gained some other way. Above all, no top man on the ULTRA list was allowed to risk capture by the enemy.

Left: an artist depicts a V-1 rocket attack on England, showing a rocket shot down by antiaircraft fire. The bombing of Peenemünde as the result of ULTRA intelligence delayed the V-1 assault for about six valuable months, giving London a chance to strengthen its defenses.

For Winterbotham, the task of laying down the law in person to such prima donnas as Major General George Patton and Major General Jimmy Doolittle was a formidable one. It did not always go smoothly. On the occasion when General Dwight D. Eisenhower and Lieutenant General Mark Clark were due for their first ULTRA briefing, Clark disbelievingly walked out on the conference after 15 minutes. Before long, however, the evidence of ULTRA was too plain to be denied by him or anyone else in the American military.

The trust the Germans steadfastly placed in their Enigma machines was to prove costly on the Eastern Front as well. By 1942 it is known that the Soviets also had cracked the secret of the cipher machine. What they learned as a result remains locked in the depths of Red Army files. But there is no doubt, as the daily warbling of secret transmitters beaming messages to Moscow from occupied Europe demonstrated, that huge quantities of intercepted signals were relayed.

In London, as the war drew to its conclusion, there were other triumphs for the dedicated code-breakers and their colleagues. One day the ULTRA team decoded a message demanding protection for the Germans' F2G 76 site on the Baltic Sea. R. V. Jones, an Air Force intelligence expert on the select list of those receiving ULTRA information, wondered if it could be a missile base. He warned the code-breakers to look out for signals moving two special companies to the place, believing that the best radar plotters of the German Army were in those companies. In due course, the companies and the radar plotters moved in. The alerted ULTRA team was able to pick up the flight paths being planned for the missiles, which turned out to be the V-1 rockets. The network of paths led to a single starting point: Peenemünde. By bombing Peenemünde, the Allies delayed the V-1 rocket program by six months.

Operation Overlord

The final and crucial contribution of ULTRA was to aid Operation Overlord, the Allied invasion of mainland Europe from the British Isles.

For the Germans, the site of the threatened invasion was a matter of intense speculation—and, fortunately for the code-breakers, some of this speculation was reflected in ULTRA messages. In 1943 the code-breakers had learned that General K. von Rundstet feared the Allies would arrive on the continent by way of Calais.

To foster that notion, the Allied powers mounted a massive

Right: Allied commanders in a planning conference for Operation Overlord, popularly known as D-Day, on February 14, 1944. General Dwight D. Eisenhower (center) later said that the contribution made by ULTRA to the success of the invasion had been "decisive." Secret German messages were in the hands of the Allies within an hour of being dispatched.

Below: that terrible, lonely, dangerous moment of a soldier going ashore on D-Day as captured by the camera of famous *Life* photographer Robert Cappa.

diversionary exercise, putting an entire ghost army opposite the far northern beaches of France. By the Spring of 1944, the ULTRA teams listened in to the high-level debate between Hitler and his hard-pressed generals on the best way to meet the powerful Allied attack.

Rommel was in favor of meeting an invasion on the beaches. General Heinz Guderian campaigned to keep his tanks well back from the sea. Delightedly the Allies learned that, in the end, the Germans took the right decision from the Allied point of view, and held their tanks back near Paris. Had they been moved up to the coast, it is doubtful if Overlord could have proceeded as planned.

For Group Captain Winterbotham, the host of military stars based on Britain for Operation Overlord demanded another swift expansion of the team that had begun life in a hut a few years before. A school in North London was converted to train 60 additional cipher sergeants for the task of keeping Allied commanders in touch during the battle ahead.

When the invasion came, the SLUs moved in with it to give their secret service on the mainland of Europe. There was a great deal of ULTRA to process as Hitler and his commanding officers fought an increasing battle of words among themselves.

By August 2, 1944 Hitler was in personal control of the war. He ordered his generals to counterattack and divide the Americans at the base of the Cherbourg peninsula.

Promptly the Allied commanders, who were receiving ULTRA messages within one hour of dispatch, regrouped. Valuable time was allowed them by General Günther von

Above: the Allies on their advance through France after D-Day. Forewarned by ULTRA, the Allies easily beat off enemy counterattacks, allowing the breakout from the beachheads.

Kluge's resistance to Hitler's demand for an attack. Even without Allied knowledge of it—a nightmare that never crossed Kluge's mind—the attack seemed hazardous to him. Grimly the messages flashed back and forth between Führer and general, each promptly read by the Allies. Three Allied armies, forewarned by ULTRA, swung into the flank of the Germans. The doomed German forces poured straight into an onslaught of Allied air power and ground artillery. Kluge's ULTRA message to Hitler was bleak: "The attack has been brought to a standstill with the loss of over half the tanks."

For the ULTRA team it was a tribute to their craft. As Eisenhower later told Winterbotham's boss, Colonel Menzies, its contribution had been "decisive."

It was by no means the end of the war, however, and the SLU network spread to the Far East, taking with them their careful patterns of security. Japan was also using modified Enigma machines. World-wide, from Australia to China, Allied commanders were obedient to the security measures laid down by Group Captain Winterbotham at the start of it all. But in Bletchley, as the European war approached an end, the ULTRA messages took on a new style. The final frenzy of the Nazi

Left: Hitler, who took personal command of the war around August 1944, confers with Nazi generals. They never knew that the British were decoding their secret messages almost as soon as they were sent.

Below: one of Hitler's personal radio operators at work. Hitler's final defiant message from the Berlin bunker, like his earlier messages, was quickly read and relayed by the ULTRA staff.

hierarchy saw the leaders deploying divisions that existed only on paper, and shifting tanks that had long been burned-out shells.

On April 15, 1945 came a final desperate cry from the heart of the Berlin bunker, a last ULTRA message from Hitler himself. Although he was preparing for suicide, he declared: "Once again Bolshevism will suffer Asia's old fate. It will founder on the capital of the Reich. Berlin stays German, Vienna will be German again, and Europe will never be Russian."

The rest was silence. For the men and women in Bletchley and the world-wide network they had created to protect the ULTRA secret, the trying task was done. Their secret, the most important and longest sustained in code-breaking, had been preserved. The experts dispersed to their colleges and universities.

Group Captain F. W. Winterbotham went quietly to farm in southwest England. He was awarded a modest decoration— a nearly anonymous prize suitable for a man who had learned to keep himself and his secrets out of the limelight. For another 30 years, until the rule of silence released him to write a book about his experiences, the story of the war by code stayed safe with him.

Revolution, Resistance, Espionage

6

Cryptology in the 20th century may hinge on machines and sophisticated techniques. But there has always been another element in the secret language of spies: a kind of cunning that can on occasion beat the system.

The scene is late-19th-century Russia. Although Czar Alexander II had abolished serfdom, the Nihilist movement felt that reforms were coming too slowly. The Nihilists were determined to overthrow the entire czarist system, and had made three attempts on Czar Alexander's life. In the first a terrorist shot point-blank at the human target and missed. The second time the terrorists blew up a train on which the czar was supposed to be traveling, and killed 20 passengers, but the czar was not on that train. The third attempt had been to dynamite the Winter Palace, which claimed 30 more lives, but again the czar managed to escape death.

General L. Melikoff, Minister of the Interior, had been placed in charge of the police department dealing with terrorists. He abandoned the use of political police in favor of infiltrating his own spies among the terrorists themselves. As a result of the new method, he eventually succeeded in capturing Gabriel Mikhailoff, who was one of the chief leaders—and possibly *the* leader—of the Nihilist movement.

Melikoff knew that Mikhailoff had been involved in the operation of the Nihilist printing presses. He decided to try to persuade the prisoner to send literature to those still running the presses. If Mikhailoff cooperated, the tracking down of other members of the group, as well as the destruction of the presses, could be achieved at a single stroke.

One of the guards let Mikhailoff know that he was secretly in favor of the Truth and Freedom Group, as this particular terrorist group was called. Another guard, feigning sympathy, managed to secure paper and pencil for him. A few days later Mikhailoff and the first guard held a hurried conversation, and a manuscript changed hands.

It quickly changed hands again, from the guard to General Melikoff. Naturally it was in cipher, but although fairly complicated, it was not beyond the capabilities of Melikoff's trained cryptanalysts. The document proved to be no more than a

Above: Alexander II, czar of Russia from 1855 to 1881. He was assassinated by political terrorists known as Nihilists. The plot for the killing had been arranged from within one of the czar's own prisons by use of a code-within-a-code that expert government cryptanalysts had failed to detect.

Right: a print of the czar's assassination, by present-day artist Flavio Constantini, an Italian anarchist. The ruler was killed by an explosion on a city street mined with bombs.

normal Nihilist propaganda newsletter, with printing instructions. Melikoff bided his time and let several similar articles go to the same destination over the next few months.

Then he pounced, rounding up a large group of Nihilists and carting them off to prison. To Melikoff's horror, a new plan to assassinate the czar was found on one of the latest prisoners. How could they have arranged this plot when their leader was in jail?

With rising panic, Melikoff set Mikhailoff free and had him followed. Mikhailoff fell for the bait and unwittingly led the police straight to the Kobyzev cheese factory, which was being used by the Nihilists as their headquarters. Mikhailoff himself escaped, but once again the police rounded up a number of terrorists. To their utter disbelief and horror they discovered that the Nihilists had mined the whole length of a street along which the czar regularly drove twice a week.

General Melikoff, fearing dismissal if he told the full story to the czar, merely begged him not to leave the palace until the police had carried out certain investigations. Alexander was not one to be deterred for so slight a reason. He set off to review the Imperial Guard as usual. He had not gone very far when a violent explosion killed two of his guards and wounded several others. He stopped his sled, got out, and walked back toward the dead and injured men, but he never reached them. A second explosion ripped through the street, and Alexander was blown to pieces.

In a frenzy of activity Melikoff's men rounded up every Nihilist they could lay their hands on. They questioned them exhaustively. It was only then that they learned that Mikhailoff, from the safety of his prison cell, had directed every move made by the Truth and Freedom Group over a period of some six months. Each of the bulky manuscripts, so willingly delivered by the police themselves, had contained a second cipher hidden within the first. Each gave detailed orders for terrorist activity. Although the Nihilists were finally destroyed, they had achieved their goal of assassinating Czar Alexander II—and a clever code had helped them do it.

No matter how clever the code, however, its success rests on the competence and judgment of both transmitter and receiver. Human error on the part of Allied receivers was to lead to the worst cryptological disaster of World War II.

In the early years of the war Hitler had invaded Denmark, Norway, Belgium, and the Netherlands in quick succession. His army took over with crushing ease, with one exception— the underground resistance movements.

To help these resistance movements, Britain established the Special Operations Executive (SOE). This military espionage service gave supplies, men, money, and information to anti-Nazi underground resistance groups. The link with these groups was by radio, and secret transmitters were set up throughout the German-occupied areas of Europe.

Above: an eyewitness drawing of the trial of the anarchists accused of the czar's murder. Gabriel Mikhailoff, seen second from the left in the prisoners' dock, was the brains of the successful plot. He masterminded it through coded messages sent from jail, which the police thought they had solved.

Right: the hanging of five of the czar's assassins. They were dressed in black hooded robes that were tied somewhat like a straitjacket. A sixth member of the plot escaped hanging because she was then pregnant.

The Nordpol Transmitter

In the Netherlands on a January day in 1942, Nazi Major Herman Giskes was told by an informer when and where the next parachute drop of radio equipment from England would take place. Giskes laughed at the informer and told him to "run to the North Pole" with such an unlikely tale. Within a few days, however, a new radio transmitter began to send out messages from The Hague. When informed of this, the General laughed at himself instead. He christened the transmitter *Nordpol* (North Pole) because of his words to the informer.

The Germans set about tracking down the transmitter, and finally located it in a street less than a mile away from their own Abwehr, or Army Intelligence Service, headquarters in The Hague.

Major Giskes planned a *funkspiel* on this transmitter. A funkspiel is equivalent to *playback* (feeding false information to the opposition while at the same time drawing out information by impersonating a captured spy on his or her radio). The Germans hoped to get enough information from London to infiltrate the underground movements, and—with luck—to learn the exact date of the Allied invasion.

On Friday March 6, 1942 four cars blocked Fahrenheitstraat. In one of the cars a radio operator tuned in to the wavelength of the underground transmitter. As soon as the transmitter came into use, the Germans broke into the house from which the signals were heard and captured Hubertus Lauwers with his transmitter and three messages.

Under interrogation Lauwers revealed how his cipher worked. But, because of his SOE training, he did not reveal all. He deliberately neglected to tell the Germans his security check. A security check was a prearranged signal that had to appear in every message transmitted by an agent. If the special signal—usually an error—did not appear, the SOE would be warned that all was not well. Lauwers was supposed to make a spelling mistake with the 16th letter of every message.

During one interrogation session he was almost caught off guard. "And what kind of mistake do you have to make?" asked Giskes. His heart thumping, Lauwers remembered the three messages that had been captured with him. It happened that in two out of the three, the 16th letter had been the *o* in the word *stop*. He quickly saw he could cover up the change of the letter by talking about a change of word. "I have to change the word *stop* once in every message to either *step* or *stip*," he said, and the Germans accepted his explanation.

Two weeks later Lauwers was ordered to transmit a message to London requesting them to change the location of the next drop from Zautkamp to Steenwijk Moor because Zautkamp was so isolated. It was his first chance to warn London. He sent the message without his security check.

Lauwers was forced to send the German messages himself on his own transmitter rather than being replaced by a German

Below: Major Herman Giskes, who worked against the Dutch resistance movement during World War II. He was chief of the highly successful counterespionage operation code-named *Nordpol* (North Pole), which captured spies and equipment being supplied by the British.

HOT AIR IN HOLLAND

Below: Hubertus Lauwers, a Dutch resistance worker caught by Giskes in The Hague. He was clever enough—and courageous enough—to figure out a way to warn London that all was not well, but although his signal was undetected by the Nazis, it was not noticed by London.

radio operator. This was done because transmitting Morse code is much like playing a musical instrument, and a change of touch can be detected by the listener. The Germans wanted to prevent such detection.

Two days later London gave the signal that the drop was to be made. Neither Lauwers nor Giskes knew for sure whether England had swallowed the last message.

The Germans, hiding in the bushes of Steenwijk Moor, heard the drone of an airplane overhead, and saw five black bundles parachute gently to earth. The delighted Germans looked at one another in amazement. The funkspiel had worked, and the promised radio supplies had been delivered.

In a way it was not too surprising that London had failed to notice the missing security check. Weak transmission signals,

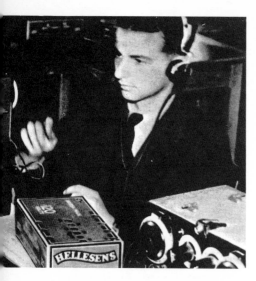

Above: the transmitting and receiving station of the SOE in Britain. Lauwer's deliberate mistakes should have been spotted by someone at this post. The failure to do so gave the Germans a decided advantage. Right: Nazis collect supplies dropped into the Netherlands by the British. Nordpol kept them fully informed of times and places of the vital drops.

bad atmospheric conditions, and jamming by the Germans frequently led to garbled messages. The best that could be expected was 95 percent clarity; most of the time London was pleased to get the message at all.

For the next seven months Lauwers continued to send messages for the Germans, each time omitting his security check. Each time London carelessly overlooked his warning and continued to play into Nazi hands.

On the basis of information from London, Giskes was able to penetrate the entire Dutch resistance movement. Station after station was turned into a funkspiel. In the end he had 14 underground radio transmitters at his disposal, which fed London with false information. To keep the English from suspecting the funkspiel, the Germans even operated a resistance group that London came to respect for its success in getting British airmen back to England. Information received from London was going straight to Hitler himself.

Lauwers was getting desperate at London's failure to pick up his warnings. At last he took a gamble and changed his tactics. By carefully selecting the letters *c, g,* and *h* for the *nulls* (symbols that mean nothing and are intended to confuse interceptors) in a message, he decided he could send the word *caught*. He trusted that the man pointing the gun at his head would not notice the deliberate error. The message that Lauwers was to transmit for the Germans was in the usual five-letter

groups. Two of the groups were as follows: CEXGI THAPE. The important letters for Lauwers were the whole of the first group and the first letter of the second group. By deliberate errors in transmission he was able to signal CAUGHT, CAUGHT, CAUGHT three times. The Nazis noticed nothing. Unfortunately, neither did London.

In March 1943 Pieter Dourlein, a new agent, was dropped into the Netherlands. Before being sent he had been instructed in the importance of omitting his security check if he were caught. His career as an agent was to be short-lived.

"For the dropping operation I had a code name, Paul," he later said. "As soon as I was on the ground I heard people calling 'Paul, Paul,' and flashing lights. I thought they were my own people sent to meet me so I pocketed my pistol and went with them to their leader. And there I was arrested.

"They took me to Driebergen for interrogation and I realized the Germans knew much more about the organization than I did. They seemed to know everything. They even asked me for my security check. I eventually told them my code and a false check. They seemed satisfied and carted me off to the Gestapo prison."

The prison in which Dourlein was incarcerated was in Haaren. He was kept in a high security room at the top of the building. By tapping on the hot water pipes, he managed to make contact with prisoners on the ground floor. Having satisfied himself that they were not working for the Germans, he tapped

Above: ruins of an RAF bomber shot down over the Netherlands after making a supply drop. Because the Nazis knew all the British movements, they waited until after a delivery to attack the aircraft, and so made a score on both points. By 1943 the Germans had captured over 15 tons of explosives, 3000 pistols, 5000 small arms, 2000 hand grenades, 75 transmitters, 300 machine guns, and at least half a million rounds of ammunition, among other things.

111

out a message. "All agents in enemy hands and prisoners at Haaren." Miraculously the message got through to London, but once again fate was against the British agents. Those in charge in London came to the conclusion that the message was a German trick, and they ignored it.

Unaware of this turn of events Dourlein determined to escape from Haaren and get back to London with a direct warning.

"In the courtyard was a sentry with a searchlight and machine gun," Dourlein recounted. "At night he would play the searchlight over the windows. So we couldn't get out on the outside. We had to get out on the inside. We climbed through the fanlight above the door into the corridor, and ran down the corridor into the lavatory where the window was situated outside the inner courtyard. We had ropes prepared to lower ourselves from the window onto a small roof and then down into the grounds out of sight. From there we had to climb over a barbed wire fence which was about 10 feet high. Outside that fence were sentries posted 200 yards apart. At every post were more searchlights, dogs, and machine guns. If it hadn't been for lots of trees we'd never have got away."

But they did. The German hue and cry lasted for several weeks because Giskes knew that one agent back in London could spell the end of Nordpol. But Dourlein lay low in a con-

Above: this seminary in Haaren was used as a prison for captured SOE agents. The arrows mark the route taken by Peter Dourlein and Johan Ubbink for their escape in August 1943.

Left: a Nazi poster offering a reward for information about Dourlein and Ubbink. The two men are described as robbers because the Germans refused to dignify them with the designation of resistance workers.

Right: Germans searching for Dourlein and Ubbink. They hunted widely for several months.

Belooning F. 500.-.

Onderstaande Personen:

Johan Bernard UBBINK
geb. 22.5.21 in DOESBURG,
laatst gewoond hebbende:
te ARNHEM,
stuurman

en

Peter DOURLEIN,
geb. 2.2.18 in VEERE,
laatst gewoondhebbende:
te AMSTERDAM,
metselaar

worden door de recherchecentrale gezocht terzake straatroof.

Ieder die inlichtingen kan verschaffen, wenden zich tot de plaatselijke politie.

vent a couple of miles away from the prison. More than three months after his escape, he finally reached England via Gibraltar. But Nordpol had told London that Dourlein was a double agent, and his reception was not what he had anticipated. The Secret Service, MI5, did not believe his story, and he was sent to prison as a German double agent. It seemed that no matter how strong the evidence was, London would ignore it.

Suspicions were finally aroused, however, and the SOE stopped sending any important information to the Netherlands. Giskes realized that Nordpol was played out. So with a wry sense of humor he arranged for all the Nordpol stations to transmit the following message on April 1, 1944:

"To Messrs. Blunt, Bingham & Co., Successors Ltd., London. We understand that you have been endeavoring for some time to do business in Holland without our assistance. We regret this the more since we have acted for so long as your sole representatives in this country, to our mutual satisfaction. Nevertheless we can assure you that, should you be thinking of paying us a visit on the continent on any extensive scale, we shall give your emissaries the same attention as we have hitherto, and a similarly warm welcome. Hoping to see you."

After nearly two years the most successful funkspiel of the war came to an end. The negligence of the London office in neither spotting nor heeding any of the warnings that were

given by courageous and clever agents is difficult to believe.

The Dutch funkspiel netted the Germans a total of 30,000 pounds of explosives, 200 hand grenades, 3000 sten guns, 5000 revolvers, 500,000 cartridges, 75 radio transmitters, and half a million Dutch guilders. But the greatest loss to the Allies was in human terms: 47 out of the 52 agents dropped over the Netherlands met their deaths at the hands of Nazi firing squads, and 1200 Dutch resistance workers were lost. All because London had not heeded its own security checks.

The Lucy Ring

Throughout the war clandestine radio transmitters were used not only in occupied territories but also in neutral countries. The Soviet spy network known as the Lucy Ring, for example, flourished in Switzerland.

The Lucy Ring was remarkably efficient. The Soviets had come to the field of cryptology late, but they had rapidly established supremacy.

One of the rules of Soviet spy networks was that no head of any group could work inside the country on which he was spying. So it was that Alexander Rado set up his ring in Switzerland, which was neutral, to spy on Germany. The base in Switzerland gave his ring the added advantage of being outside the reach of the German Abwehr.

Rado, whose code-name was "Dora," was a Swiss cartographer then living in Geneva. He arranged any necessary meetings with other members of the ring in the streets and cafés of Geneva, but he preferred to send messages by courier or a *cutout* (go-between in clandestine work). In this way the anonymity of those in the ring was preserved.

One of Rado's earliest recruits was another Swiss by the name of Otto Punter, known as "Packbo." Punter once said:

"A ring can only exist safely if only three people know each other. This was the error in the French resistance. In the beginning everybody knew everybody else and if one of them was caught, all of them were caught. If you don't know the name of anybody you can't give them away to the police."

Another of Rado's recruits was the first of two radio operators that the ring had. He was Edmund Hammel, otherwise "Edward." Hammel ran a small radio store in Geneva, but broadcast his transmissions to the Soviet Union from his own home on the outskirts of the city. In order to let Rado know when it was safe to enter his store by a side door, Hammel put a clock in the window. If the time it showed was correct, it was safe to enter; if the clock had stopped at noon, it was not.

The information that the Lucy Ring supplied to the Soviet Union in the early days was mostly details of industrial output in southern Germany. It was only when a small bespectacled German immigrant was brought into the ring that the information became of almost dazzling importance.

Rudolf Roessler, whose code-name "Lucy" derived from the fact that he lived in Lucerne, was a German publisher. Early in the war he had informed the Swiss Secret Service of the exact dates of the German invasions of Poland, the Netherlands, Belgium, and Denmark. This information had been passed to the Allies, who had doubted its truth. From then on Roessler worked for the Soviet Union.

Hammel and Punter were, as everyone else was to be, astounded at the quality of Lucy's information. "The information from Roessler was so fantastic and precise that it was really not easy to believe it," said Punter. "To give you an example—when Hitler decided to attack Russia. Well, 10 days before this happened, Dora [Rado] came to me and said, 'I've a vital message which must go out this evening without fail because it says Hitler will attack Russia in a week.'"

The chief radio operator for the ring was a young Englishman, an immigrant who was said to have moved to Switzerland to avoid conscription. His name was Alexander Foote, and he lived in an apartment at 2 chemin de Longeraie in Lausanne. He and his radio station were always referred to as "Jim."

When Foote first began to work for Rado he was in contact with the Soviets about twice a week. In June 1941 he sent out the following message: "Dora to Director, via Taylor. Hitler has definitely set June 22 for attack on Russia."

Stalin, who was disinclined to believe any information that came to him from outside his own country, curtly dismissed the message.

On June 22, 1941 the Nazis invaded the Soviet Union.

From that day, Foote maintained around-the-clock contact with the Soviets. The messages he sent and received fell into three categories. The prefix MSG meant routine; RDO, urgent; and VYRDO, extremely urgent. Lucy's messages were invariably sent as VYRDO.

115

For two years Foote worked almost ceaselessly. His schedule was grueling. He enciphered messages during the evening and transmitted them to the Center in Moscow in the early hours of the morning. After a few hours of sleep he rose again at 10:00 a.m. to play his role as an English immigrant. He spent the afternoons meeting couriers and gathering the useful information that Moscow needed.

"I usually had a long evening's ciphering before me. According to the rules, all ciphering should have been done after dark and behind locked doors. But needs must when the Center drove, and in more hectic times I was enciphering in all my spare moments."

The cipher used by the Lucy Ring was a three-step cipher. The Soviets always enciphered their messages in English in order to throw others off the scent.

The Lucy cipher was based on the phrase "a sin to er" because 60 percent of English words can be written using just these letters. Each letter was assigned a number as follows:

```
0 1 2 3 4 5 6 7
A S I N T O E R
```

The rest of the alphabet was placed under these letters in two lines to form a square, with the addition of a period, a blank, the number 8, and the number 9. It then looked like this:

Above: German tanks rolling into the Soviet Union after their surprise attack. Lucy had informed the Soviets of the German plan to invade—even to the exact date—but Stalin refused to believe it.

Right: Alexander Foote, chief radio operator for the Lucy Ring, was the one who transmitted Roessler's message to Stalin about the German invasion. Pictured in London in the late 1950s, he had lived in Switzerland during the war.

116

	0	1	2	3	4	5	6	7	8	9
	A	S	I	N	T	O	E	R		
8	B	C	D	F	G	H	J	K	L	M
9	P	Q	U	V	W	X	Y	Z	.	/

The letters in the first row (ASINTOER) were represented by the single numbers above them. The rest of the alphabet was written as number pairs starting with the number at the side followed by the number at the top. A message was enciphered in this way:

H I T L E R H A S D E F I N I TE L Y
85 2 4 88 6 7 85 0 1 82 6 83 2 3 2 4 6 88 96

These numerals were then condensed into the normal groups of five: 85248, 86785, 01826, 83232, and so on.

The next stage of enciphering involved the use by both encipherer and decipherer of identical books of statistics. A page, and a line and a column on that page, were taken at random. The column of numbers was strung out in a left-to-right line, such as 132217098443801. These were also grouped into fives, added to the enciphered groups of figures, and totaled to create a new group of figures, as follows:

Code Group	85248	86785	01826
Statistic Book	*13221*	*70984*	*43801*
Total	98469	57769	45627

These totals were the groups of figures that were transmitted.

In order to inform the recipient which page, line, and column were to be used, a number was formed embodying them. For example, column 13, line 3, page 57 became 13357. A prearranged five-figure group was then added, say 45627. The new group was then:

$$45627$$
$$13357$$
$$58984$$

This five-digit number, 58984, was then inserted into the message at a prearranged spot, perhaps as the sixth group. Each line, column, and page in the book was used only once.

The Lucy Ring decided that statistics books were too bulky and swapped to ordinary books, turning the letters of the alphabet into numbers in reverse order so that A became 26 and Z became 1. The key group was in the order of line, starting word, page. Although both the Swiss and the Germans intercepted hundreds of Lucy messages they could not break this code.

The length of time it took Foote to transmit his messages varied widely. "My transmission time was usually about one in the morning," he said. "If conditions were good and the messages were short I was through in about a couple of hours. If, as frequently happened, I had long messages to send and atmospherics were bad I had to fight my way through and send when and as conditions allowed. Often on such occasions I was still at the transmitter at six and once or twice I 'signed off' at nine in the morning. . . . To be on the air for that length of time broke all the normal precautions against radio monitoring. But it was a chance which had to be taken if the intelligence was to be passed

over, a risk which the Center took despite frequent admonitions by Rado and me."

One night when Foote was taking down a message from Moscow the Center suddenly went off the air without warning. Every day for the next few nightmarish weeks Rado and Foote called Moscow repeatedly. To no avail.

"Night after night Rado and I called, and night after night there was no reply. Rado was in despair and talked of going over to the British." Then as abruptly as they had gone off the air, they came back on. "One night at the scheduled time—and six weeks after the break—the Center piped up. As if nothing had happened they finished the message that they had cut off half-way through, a month and a half before."

What had happened? As the Germans approached Moscow, someone in command had without prior warning to the radio operators ordered the whole of the Center to vacate Moscow instantly. Six weeks later they were installed some 550 miles away in a place named Kuibyshev, and resumed operation as though they had never been interrupted.

After two years the Swiss Secret Service got wind of the fact that the Nazis were determined to send special agents into Switzerland to track down and destroy the transmitters that were so successfully sending signals to the Soviet Union. The Swiss decided to beat the Nazis to it, as much to retain their neutrality as anything.

Lucy and the Battle of Kursk

The battle between 1500 German and Soviet tanks at Prochorovka in July 1943 was among the bloodiest of any in World War II. The huge steel machines of war proved to be a hellish grave for hundreds of Nazi soldiers, and their defeat put an end to the Nazi design of overrunning the Soviet Union.

The Soviet victory depended on preparedness for the Nazi offensive, and the fact that Hitler postponed the attack three times was of great help in allowing the Soviets to mass their forces on the Kursk front. The Soviets' secret weapon was the intelligence about Nazi plans provided by one of the masterminds of World War II espionage: Rudolf Roessler, code-named Lucy. He worked from Switzerland, and the information he supplied was of remarkable accuracy. In fact it was of such quality, and obtained so quickly after Nazi policy decisions were made, that it was believed his source must be a high-placed figure from within Germany—perhaps an anti-Hitler general.

Lucy kept the Soviets informed of all Hitler's directives. On April 15, 1943 Hitler sent a top-secret message giving the new date for "Operation Citadel," the campaign on the Eastern Front. He said in part: "It is largely a question of sustaining the moment of surprise and above all leaving the opponent in the dark about the time of the attack . . . not until June or July. . . ." Only five days later, Lucy had taken any surprise out of Hitler's plan by informing the Soviets of the delay.

More than that, Lucy was also able to answer such direct questions from Soviet military leaders as: at what point on the south sector of the Eastern Front will the German offensive actually begin? with what forces and in which direction will the advance be led? what day will the attack take place?

When Nazi tanks finally attacked at Prochorovka on July 10, the Soviets had already dug a maze of trenches, built many bunkers, and mined miles of fields. The Germans were rolled back in a furious Soviet counterassault.

The Battle of Kursk was one of the biggest tank battles in history, and the Soviet victory helped change the course of the war.

Left: German tanks advancing on Kursk, about 300 miles southwest of Moscow, in 1943. This time the Nazis were stopped in their tracks by Soviet forces forewarned and prepared for an attack by information given by Roessler.

Their method was ingenious. They were fairly certain that the transmitter based in Geneva was using electricity off the mains. They therefore cut the power in different sections of the city until they hit the one that made the transmitter go dead. They then restored the power, and using direction-finding equipment, swooped on Hammel and arrested him. The Swiss intelligence had papers that included the cover names of the other agents, and also had copies of messages both in plaintext and in cipher. They soon realized that another transmitter based in Lausanne was sending out similar messages.

In the early hours of November 20, 1943 Foote was in the middle of taking a message from Moscow. In Foote's words: "There was a splintering crash and my room was filled with police. . . . I was arrested and the last link between the Center and Switzerland was broken."

Where did Lucy get his information? The secret went with him to his grave. But theories abound. One says that old friends of his were top Nazi generals—among them perhaps Martin Bormann—who beamed the information to him directly. Another holds that the Ultra machine in London had picked up the information, and that Churchill had passed it on via Lucy because Stalin would not listen to him.

Lucy was certainly one of the most effective and brilliant spies World War II produced. And the unbreakable code of the Lucy Ring holds a special place in cryptologic history.

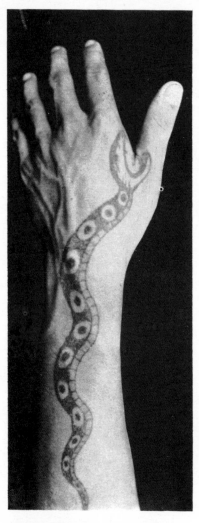

Above: this tattoo identifies the bearer as a member of the Triad, a Chinese secret society. This particular sign is that of the Singapore "108" group.

Criminal Codes

7

On May 28, 1976 a slim and youthful Chinese stepped out of a British Airways plane that had just arrived at London's Heathrow airport from Hong Kong. No one would guess that he was a police superintendent on an undercover job for Scotland Yard. His name was Lau Yuk-Kuen, and at the age of 29 he was one of the few experts on the Triad—the powerful and menacing Chinese crime syndicate of international scope.

Lau's destination was Gerrard Street, a short and narrow street in the entertainment district of London known as Soho, just east of the bright lights of Shaftesbury Avenue. In 10 years, this 200-yard-long street had burgeoned into one of the most important Chinatowns of Europe. At first there were only restaurants, but later the community developed its own newspapers, supermarkets, social clubs, and schools. The Chinese New Year celebration in winter became for Londoners an exciting and colorful day out, with a traditional parade along the lantern-hung street. But in 1976 Gerrard Street also acquired something sinister: the Triad.

The Triad is an ancient organization whose roots are lost in the distant past. Today, however, it is unchallenged as a world-

Above: the Chinese New Year celebration on Gerrard Street, London. An invasion of London's Chinatown by the Triad in 1976 was successfully repelled by Scotland Yard with the help of a Hong Kong detective. Whatever its roots as a society of social and political protest, the present-day Triad is concerned with crime.

wide crime syndicate even more ruthless and violent than the Mafia. Its leaders and its activities are protected by a network of secrecy, including a highly evolved code system of signs and symbols. Part of this is sign language that resembles deaf-mute gestures. A Triad member can signal when a fee has been paid or received, point out silently someone who has been in the pay of the society, or communicate many other facts. Lau was one of the few law enforcement officers familiar with the operation and codes of the Triad. He was needed in London to help Scotland Yard prevent the syndicate from getting a stranglehold on Gerrard Street.

In Hong Kong Lau had succeeded in making inroads on this formidable organization. In 1973 he masterminded a major attack on the Triad community in an operation code-named *Halam*. Ironically, the very success of that cleanup led to the London problem that Lau had been invited to solve. Chased out of Hong Kong, the Triad looked across several continents to the thriving Chinatown of Gerrard Street, and moved in on it.

In the winter of 1975 Kan Wong was kicked to death in a Gerrard Street gambling house. He had been a restaurant owner,

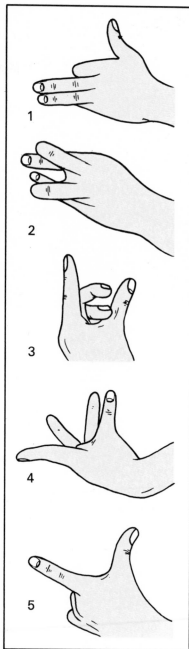

and it was a revenge killing. At this point Scotland Yard began to get worried enough to study the intricate network of international Triad operations. It was the Chinese community itself that most forcefully put the case for immediate action. "If the police would only come in now and make arrests this trouble could be stopped," said one community leader. "But if they let it go on much longer it will get too big. We need help."

The law-abiding and friendly Chinese community of Gerrard Street began to talk quietly about the "new men" who were coming in from Hong Kong. They and the police agreed on what might happen next: a takeover of London's drug smuggling by brutal racketeers. Up till then Britain's organized crime had traditionally kept to old-fashioned if sophisticated robberies, the protection racket, and straightforward gang warfare. With the Triad, however, came a real danger that drug trafficking, which was better controlled in Britain because addicts could get help under the National Health Service, would fall into the hands of professional criminals as it had done in the United States.

That was when the British police called in Superintendent Lau. They were depending on him to help them crack the secret code of the Triad.

Thieves' Cant

Crime has always depended on secrecy, and criminals have long used codewords and codes. Crooked businessmen, organizers of call girl rackets, crime syndicates, and the ordinary petty thief—all have made code language a part of their illegal activities.

Criminal codewords are an almost international language of the underworld. The earliest usage seems to have stemmed from argot, a slang language in common use in medieval Europe. Most of the argot vocabulary is now lost, but in all probability many of the words simply had a double meaning. An Elizabethan instruction manual for thieves stresses the importance of slang. It says: "These Babes of Grace [young thieves] should be taught by a master well verst in the cant language or slang patter, in which they shall by all means excel."

By the early 19th century, underworld slang had reached a stage where it was possible for confederates in crime to hold a conversation in front of strangers without revealing a single clue as to the actual content of their conversation. From that stage, argot became more and more complex in order to deal with the ever widening variety of crime. In the end it became necessary for criminals to learn mnemonic rhymes to jog their memories, and argot went into a decline. Its demise as a practical language was hastened by the rise of trained police forces whose members found ways to learn the underworld language.

Coded messages of any complexity are rarely necessary in the crime world. But codewords and code systems have a definite place. For more than 20 years, for example, Frank Costello

of the Mafia operated a simple code system that worked effectively. Aware that his mail was under constant FBI surveillance, Costello let it be known to those to whom he wrote that anything he said meant the exact opposite. If he said that he was going to Boston, he was not going to Boston. If he recommended that someone be encouraged, he was ordering that he or she be discouraged with all the customary care. The FBI searched in vain for some subtle code in the letters, never discovering the simplicity of the system.

Mafia codewords refer to many aspects of the organization. "The arm" has long denoted the great Buffalo crime family, just as "the office" denotes the New England counterpart. To be "on the arm" is to be on credit, and an organization that is "on the pad" is paying regular bribes.

"Made guys" of the Mafia are its members. They may be "head hunters" (assassins), "mechanics" (the gambling games riggers), "right arms" (the underbosses), or "stone killers" (the professional murderers). Together these racketeers conduct their continual warfare with "Uncle Sugar" (the FBI). In their warfare the tools of the trade are "biscuits" (guns), and anyone in

Above: prisoners, many of them drug addicts, await their supper in Hong Kong's Tai Lam jail. When the police made inroads on Triad control of the illegal drugs traffic, the organization tried to broaden its area of operation to London.

123

conflict with them may "have the X put on them" (be designated
for murder). Should the proposed victims succeed in avoiding
"a serious headache" (a bullet in the head) by "hitting the
mattress" (going into hiding), they still risk the "shiv" (knife).
Traditional and long-standing as much of the Mafia codeword
list is, modern additions often show a contempt for the older
generation. An old Italian or Sicilian is more likely than not to
be referred to as a "greaseball." The elder statesmen of the
original Mafia in the United States are called "mustache Petes."

Like other criminals, Mafia members get caught and are im-
prisoned. The prison world they and others enter has its own
code jargon, much of which dates back for centuries. British
prison codewords and coded signals derive from the old tradition
of Cockney slang—for example, "twirls" denotes the guards'
keys, and "snout" the tobacco that is usually the principal
currency in any prison.

There are silent signals, too. A man emerging from the
lavatory and briefly tapping his nose will more likely than not be
informing a watchful colleague that some snout has been
planted inside for collection. A quickly bent finger pointing at

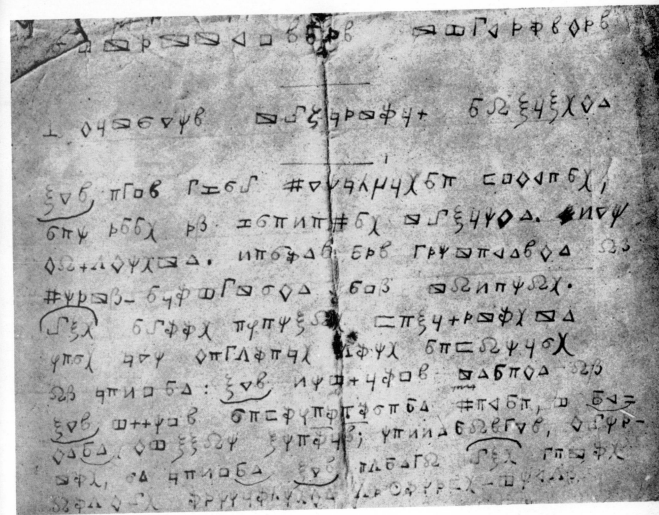

the ground will signify that a particular guard is "crooked," and therefore will probably be open to bribery for favors.

Before criminals adapted the products of modern technology to their use, they had a complex system of picture codes. A story about Hans Gross, who became one of Germany's top criminologists, points this up. One December day in the early part of this century, Gross was passing through a village in Austria close to the Hungarian border. He happened to notice a crude sketch on one of the church walls. Intrigued, he took a closer look—and immediately headed for the village police station. He told the police that if they were to keep a lookout on Christmas Day, they would probably see two or three strangers loitering around the church. These strangers would be planning a breakin for the following day, he assured the astounded police. The police did as he suggested, and to their delight captured three of the most wanted criminals on their books.

How had Gross known the criminals' plans? Once they had been caught, he was happy to explain.

"It is all written on the wall of the chapel," he said. "The first drawing is the crude sketch of a parrot, made in a single line.

Above: an illustration from an article on ciphers in the *Illustrated London News*, **August 25, 1928. It is a** *steganogram* **(a secret alphabet composed of hieroglyphs and Greek letters) found on a dangerous safe-cracker of that period.**

The fact that it has been made in this way means that it is the signature of a criminal, and the sketch itself indicates that he is known as 'The Parrot.' The drawing of a church means just that, and the key beside it signifies that the church is to be 'unlocked' or robbed. The drawing below is a crude representation of an infant in swaddling clothes. I assumed that this meant Christmas Day; and the three stones are a symbol taken from a popular farmers' almanac and standing for St Stephen, who was stoned to death. St Stephen's Day is December 26; therefore the meaning of the whole thing is: 'The Parrot is going to burgle a church on December 26. He wants someone to help him. Anyone who is willing, meet him near here on Christmas Day when the arrangements will be made.'" When confronted with this piece of evidence, the luckless trio admitted that it was true.

Rum Running

The greatest boom in the use of codes and ciphers by the criminal element of society came in the United States as a result of Prohibition. For 13 years it was illegal to import, manufacture, sell, or consume liquor. Small-time gangs of bootleggers joined forces to form enormous syndicates, which in their own way were as powerful as any big business. They supplied the steady demand for alcohol by smuggling.

Smuggling liquor into the country was by no means an easy task, but with speak-easies mushrooming and ordinary people gladly paying exorbitant prices to drink in them, it was a quick way to large profits.

The most famous of the smuggling schooners was the *I'm Alone*. It caused a political incident that greatly embarrassed the United States government.

The *I'm Alone* had been built in 1924, to carry liquor legitimately, and registered as Canadian. It changed hands in 1928 and proceeded to ply the 1000-mile route from Belize, capital of British Honduras, to the United States. The cargo was obtained from the Melhado Brothers, among the largest liquor traders in British Honduras.

Not daring to enter United States territorial waters, the *I'm Alone* kept out of reach of the Coast Guard by anchoring just over 12 miles from the coast. The Coast Guard was certain that the schooner was running liquor, and fairly sure that it was owned by an American, despite its Canadian flag. But it was difficult to prove this. Continually on the alert, the Coast Guard followed the schooner's every move and waited to intercept ship-to-shore radio messages. There were none. The boat's owners cunningly sent all their messages direct from Belize to New York by ordinary Western Union Telegraph cables, and used accepted commercial codes.

One spring day in 1929 the Coast Guard cutter *Wolcott* challenged the *I'm Alone* to heave to. The *I'm Alone* refused, and instead turned to make a run to sea. According to the captain of the *Wolcott* the schooner was just within the boundary of United States territorial waters. The captain of the *I'm Alone* declared that he was three miles outside the limit, off the coast of Louisiana.

The chase began. It was three days before the Coast Guard finally caught up with the smuggling boat some 220 miles out, well beyond the jurisdiction of American law. Once again it was ordered to stop.

"I ordered the master of the *I'm Alone* to stop his vessel, indicating that I wished to board him," the Coast Guard captain said. "And he indicated that he would not do so. These messages continued on for some little time, sometimes by semaphore signals. But it became clear that the captain had no intention of stopping and I fired a blank or saluting shot at the bow. I believe I fired several of these shots. And no change of attitude apparently on the part of the skipper of the *I'm Alone*. So we just had to use the force we had, which was gunfire, and I directed my shells in through the hull, just above the water line. It was a long time before I brought myself to firing below the water line. But eventually I had to do that. The last shell that was fired tore a large hole in her side and she settled quickly then. And went down."

The Canadian government was furious, and demanded an apology for the sinking of the Canadian-registered boat. The Canadians also wanted $386,000 compensation for the loss of the boat and its cargo.

The Americans insisted that the boat was American-owned, and alleged that because it had been challenged in territorial waters and the chase that followed had been continuous, they were within the letter of the law to sink it—even though both boats were by then far out into international waters. In the end the United States made an apology and paid a token sum for insulting the Canadian flag.

It was not until five years after this incident that the United States government found out who actually had owned *I'm Alone*. Success came about through Elizebeth Friedman, one of the greatest American cryptanalysts, who had been working with the Coast Guard for some years. While working on a case in Houston in 1929, she had decoded more than 20 messages that had nothing to do with the case in question. She later handed them over to customs officials.

"The cable addresses used were CARMELHA for cables sent to Belize and MOCANA for cables to New York," Mrs. Friedman said. "It was just almost too obvious that Carmelha was a pronounceable number of letters made up from C. A. Melhado Brothers, the people who supplied all the liquor in Belize, British Honduras. Then I started to think about the cable address Mocana. And it seemed to me that the New York cables were obviously meant ultimately for Montreal, Canada. Mo Cana."

One such message read:

HBA69 6 Wireless—NS Belize BH 29 427p
MOCANA
NEW YORK

YODVY RYKIP PAHNY KOWAG JAJHA FYNIG IKUMV

Elizebeth Friedman recognized that this message was written
in one of the established commercial codes. Out of this came:
"blank solve repairing her not nearly must leave feasible." It did
not take the cryptanalyst long to realize that the message had
been encoded by moving down five places for each code group.
When read that way the message made sense. It said: "Arrived.
Some repairs necessary. Will leave Feb 2. Telegraph instructions." Obviously a rum runner—but which one?

The clue was the Belize dateline. The United States Consul
in Belize had taken great care to log the exact amount of liquor
loaded onto any suspect boats, together with their dates of
sailing. A look at his records revealed that the boat that left
Belize on February 2 was none other than the *I'm Alone*, and the
value of the amount of liquor on board tallied with the Canadian
government's demand for compensation. A little research
revealed that the cable address MOCANA belonged to a New-

Above: the schooner *I'm Alone*, a runner during Prohibition, under surveillance by the Coast Guard. A cryptanalyst helped the United States government prove that the schooner was owned by an American, a fact that was in dispute by Canada.

Left: a customs officer pours away barrels of illegal beer during Prohibition. The Coast Guard felt that it was simply enforcing the law when it sank the *I'm Alone* to destroy the cargo of liquor from Honduras.

York-based bootlegger, Dan Hogan, who also had an address in Canada. Hogan ran a million-dollar smuggling syndicate. The chief prosecution witness was to be Hogan's speedboat operator, Big Jim Clarke. But before the case could be heard Clarke was shot, and Hogan was already in prison on other charges.

Elizabeth Friedman had been temporarily assigned to the Coast Guard in 1928, and had worked on hundreds of coded messages that they had intercepted. She dealt with over 12,000 messages in three years.

This volume of messages was caused by the necessity for schooners smuggling liquor to make contact with the speedboats that took their cargo ashore, and to inform their shore contact when it was on the way. The rum runners had become more adept at physical evasion of the Coast Guard. They sent out decoy speedboats, for example, or dropped their stern lights attached to a buoy overboard as a false scent for the Coast Guards to follow. The Coast Guard retaliated by deciphering their coded radio messages and taking swift action on the basis of what they learned from them. In the beginning the rum runners relied on only two basic codes, which were changed infrequently—perhaps once a year. Soon, however, their cipher systems became extremely complex. By mid-1930 practically every boat involved in smuggling liquor had its own code with which to contact the mother ship. The mother ship had its own codes for sending messages to land bases and to the boats.

"The whole operation was extremely professional and the operators highly security conscious," a Coast Guard once explained. "For one thing they never, ever put any plaintext in their messages. One message I remember coming from shore to one of the ships at sea said: 'Inform second mate wife has given birth to twins.' And back came the message all duly encoded in cipher, two or three or four or five stages: 'Second mate has no wife.' It was a laugh, but they'd been careful to put it in code."

The Consolidated Exporters Corporation, a major smuggling syndicate, used a code system that was exceedingly well thought out and went through no less than four separate stages. The first step was to put the plaintext into the ABC Commercial Code, a numerical code, and the second was to add the number 1000 to each of the words so encoded. Stage three involved a second commercial code book, this time the ACME, in which letters equivalent to the numbers were to be found. For instance, 53725 became OIJYS in ACME Code. The final stage was to encipher these letters using a monalphabetic (a one-cipher alphabet) substitution.

Mrs Friedman gives the following example of part of a four-stage coded message she unraveled:

	plain	Anchored in	harbor.
ABC		07033	52725
+1000		08033	53725
ACME		BARHY	OIJYS
Subst		MJFAK	ZYWKH

"In this case an inspection determined that the system employed came under the general classification of Enciphered Code. Then began what seemed endless experimentation to determine the particular type of enciphered code. There are hundreds of public codes any one of which might have been used, and in order to discover which, it was necessary to solve the cipher applied. With enormous difficulty the cipher alphabet was built up, by which the groups actually appearing in the messages were resolved into codegroups of the ACME Code. But as this resulted in no intelligible meaning, it was obvious that further steps were necessary in order to reach clear language. The processes of experiment continued, the search among hundreds of code books was again prosecuted, and finally the whole laborious process was revealed."

Elizebeth Friedman's greatest personal success involved the breakup of the Consolidated Exporters Corporation, one of the two giants in the bootlegging industry. Her solutions to intercepted messages were used as evidence against the masterminds of the ring, which had smuggled millions of dollars worth of whiskey into the country. The messages that had been sent to rum runners such as *The Rosita, The Albert, Concord,* and *Quiatchouan* made clear the links between them and the ringleaders. One such message said: "SUBSTITUTE 50 CANADIAN CLUB BALANCE BLUE GRASS FOR COROZAL STOP REPEAT TUESDAY WIRE CONCORD GO TO LATITUDE 29.50 LONGITUDE 87.44."

After a five-day trial, five of the accused were convicted. Mrs Friedman had the satisfaction of knowing her work had destroyed one of the largest and most successful smuggling rings of the Prohibition era.

Codes used by criminals vary in their complexity. On one occasion in the mid-1950s dope smugglers coming from Bahrain to Britain by air sent a wire that read: "ORDERING 19 COULD MANAGE MORE IF AVAILABLE." This meant: "Arriving Bahrain 19 could carry more opium than previous journey." Heroin smugglers in the States use the Universal Trade Code for their messages, but to avoid detection they alter them slightly by moving the middle digit of the five-digit code to the beginning.

An Austrian art dealer with a side business had his own code to inform his customers. Police grew suspicious when they realized that his shop drew more people than the food stores. They discovered that he made frequent telephone calls to his customers to let them know when a particular "rococo statue" or "baroque angel" was ready for their inspection or collection—but the baroque angel and the rococo statue in this case proved in fact to be call girls.

One bank in Haifa was almost caught out by its own code, which was intended for legitimate use. A young employee who knew the code opened a couple of bank accounts in Switzerland, putting them under numbers rather than his name. He then

Above: William and Elizebeth Friedman in 1958 with part of their cipher machine collection. Both of the Friedmans were noted cryptanalysts who were frequently called upon for help by the government. It was while on a different assignment for the Coast Guard that Elizebeth Friedman decoded messages leading to the *I'm Alone*'s owner.

instructed three banks in the United States to pay large sums of money into these accounts. He gave these instructions in his bank's private code to avoid suspicion of his actions. On his next visit to Switzerland, he drew out $150,000. However, he was arrested when he went to collect the balance from his other account.

Luckily for the bank in Haifa, the three American banks—surprised by the unexpected demands for money to be transferred to Switzerland—sent a confirmation cable. It had arrived after the hopeful thief had left Haifa, so he could not know his scheme had been discovered.

Sometimes it takes split-second thinking to put a message into code, and a recent case in Brazil shows how it can be done. When Ronald Biggs, one of the British Great Train Robbers, was being hustled into a police car, a voice in the crowd called out: "The address has changed, Ron. It's no longer 100 Grand Avenue, Clacton; it's now 3 Grand Avenue."

This anonymous coded signal, as quickly understood by Biggs as it was delivered by the person who gave it, told Biggs a sad story. It meant that his share of the robbery had been reduced from £100,000 to £3000.

131

Is There an Unbreakable Code?

8

Millions of years from now, Pioneer 10—launched in 1972—will enter the planetary system of another star in the immense universe. On board this spacecraft is a gold-anodized aluminum plaque etched with a message from earth. That message is in code.

The code consists of symbols and drawings, and would tax the talents of many a skilled decoder. But it is expected that a scientifically and technologically advanced race from outer space will be able to make it out in the distant future. To those interceptors of superior intelligence, the plaque will reveal when Pioneer 10 was launched, where it was sent from, and what kind of beings created it.

This example of the use of code shows how all-pervading the art of codes and ciphers is today. It is an instance of a code deliberately designed to be broken. But much more importance is usually placed on rendering codes unbreakable. Take this case.

A red box lies in a room deep under the ground in the Midwest of the United States. Two men guard it day and night. Inside is a sealed message in code from the president.

A plane flies high above the earth, far from the underground room. It is one of a fleet of aircraft that, because each plane reflects what goes on in the underground post, is called the Looking Glass. One plane of the Looking Glass is always in the air. This airborne craft contains a duplicate red box, and only two of the crew have access to it. They alone can decode the president's message in the all-important red box.

The code for the president's order is changed often and without notice, but those few charged with decoding are always informed of the new code. They must be. The message in the red box might be the dreaded order for a nuclear holocaust. No wonder such effort is made to keep it from being broken.

The Unbreakable Code

Is there an unbreakable code? Have the sophisticated cryptologists in the black chambers of today achieved the dream of their many forerunners?

One way to make a code or cipher unbreakable, of course, is to

Right: this message in code is etched on a plaque that is on board the Pioneer 10 spacecraft. Pioneer 10 is headed for the universe beyond the earth's own solar system, and may one day millions of years in the future be intercepted and recovered by a technologically advanced people of outer space. They should be able to decode the message, which will tell them when, where, and by whom Pioneer 10 was launched.

Below: Pioneer 10 in action.

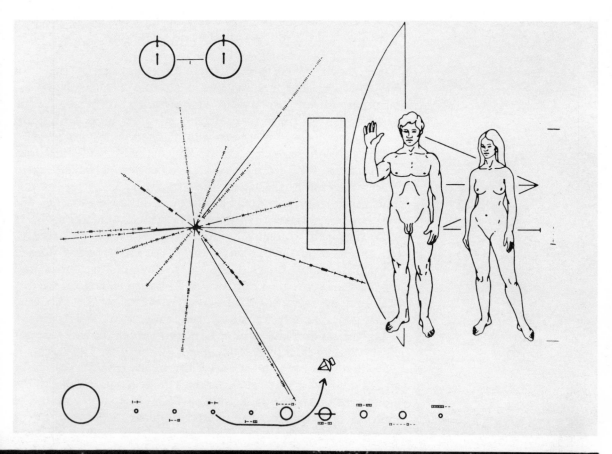

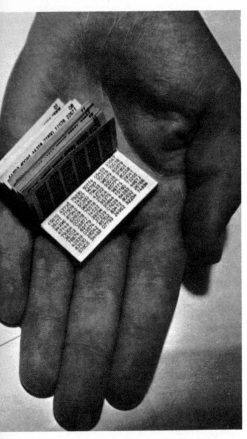

Above: the one-time pad found in the possession of Helen and Peter Kroger, two members of a spy ring caught in England in 1961. Messages enciphered by means of one-time pads, which give random coding numbers, are almost unbreakable. Encoder and decoder have duplicate pads, each sheet of which is destroyed after use.

keep it totally secret. But this way is open to human error as well as to plain old-fashioned theft—and these days theft is often made easier by technological aids.

The Soviets have a reputation for espionage by theft. In Moscow no major embassy has been able to offset KGB infiltration entirely. Embassy raids, authorized in person by the Communist Party Secretary, have sometimes been daring, but just as often have simply been well planned.

For example, in a raid on the Swedish embassy while most members of staff were away at a reception, a female agent successfully lured a night watchman from his post by her charms. The ferocious embassy dog likewise succumbed to a lure: he was fed generous portions of prime beef by a KGB officer. KGB cars were stationed strategically around the embassy, prepared to ram the car of anyone returning early. The technicians unlocked the embassy and burgled the safes, then photographed and replaced the contents. Only the KGB officer in charge of the dog had anxious moments. "This dog is eating by the kilo," he signaled desperately, "send me some more meat."

Only the most naive assume that comparable activities are not carried out by their own countries.

So theft can break most codes. But in any case the search for an unbreakable code as such is now a preoccupation more of the amateur than of the professional. Today the sheer volume of material encoded and enciphered requires a totally different perspective on the task. For instance, on August 8, 1945 Washington's War Department handled some 9.5 million words in the course of a single day. In the information-packed world of the late 1970s, that volume has been multiplied out of all proportion. The systems for handling such volumes must be swift, and must also be adapted to sophisticated electronic transmission and reception.

Besides, an unbreakable code does exist, as long as it too is not stolen or intercepted. It is known as the "one-time pad."

The one-time pad system was used successfully by master spies Lona and Morris Cohen from the late 1950s until the day they were captured near London in 1961. Born in the United States of Czechoslovakian origins, the Cohens arrived in England as Helen and Peter Kroger of New Zealand. Peter Kroger bought a secondhand-book shop on a busy thoroughfare of London.

The choice of bookselling as a cover for espionage activities was a good one. It enabled the Krogers to travel to Book Fairs throughout Europe, including those in Dresden, East Germany, and other Iron Curtain countries. Kroger could send and receive books from any country in the world without arousing suspicion. Perhaps even more important in view of the time it takes to encipher messages with a one-time pad, he could take work home. With valuable antiquarian books in the house, it was logical for the Krogers to put padlocks on all windows and doors, and alarms all around the house.

USING A ONE-TIME PAD

P	o	l	a	r	i	s	m	i	s	s	i	l	e	s	a	t
11	12	15	26	9	18	8	14	18	8	8	18	15	22	8	26	7

30221	65995	86939	40247
44094	61848	50561	06858
66239	38276	62556	59183
91030	44918	74862	46386
02706	96535	77142	12544
82463	87363	33092	27321
36844	78364	12336	38096

P	o	l	a	r	i	s
11	12	15	26	9	18	8
30221	65995	86939	40247	44094	61848	50561
30232	66007	86954	40273	44103	61866	50569

m	i	s	s	i	l	e	s
14	18	8	8	18	15	22	8
06858	66239	38276	62556	59183	91030	44918	74862
06872	66257	38284	62564	59201	91045	44940	74870

a	t
26	7
46386	02706
46412	02713

What is the one-time pad and what makes it almost infallible? It is exactly what its name says: a pad or booklet containing a number of pages. No two pages are the same, and no two pads are alike except that they are done in double sets for the encoder and decoder to use. A different sheet is used for every message, and that sheet is torn off and destroyed by the encoder when he has finished writing the dispatch and by the decoder when he has read it. The one-time pad can be as small as a postage stamp. It can also be in the form of a scroll that is about the thickness of an ordinary pencil when rolled up. It is made of highly inflammable cellulose nitrate film that can be destroyed quickly and easily in an emergency.

Above: one-time pad encoding. Each letter of the message (top) has been given a number arrived at by going backward through the alphabet with A equal to 26 and Z to 1. The numbers from a single sheet of a one-time pad (center) are taken one by one in a vertical or horizontal sequence agreed in advance, and added to the number substitute for each letter (last three lines). The number transmitted is the total of these two figures.

Above: Peter Kroger, member of the Portland Ring in England who later proved to be a long-sought-after soviet spy known as Cohen. His cover as a secondhand bookseller was useful for unsuspicious travel and mailing around the world.

Each sheet contains a random key in the form of five-digit groups, and no key is ever repeated. The first stage in enciphering is to break down the message into individual letters and substitute prearranged numbers for them. For example, the words *Polaris missiles at* could be enciphered by giving each letter a number that has been arrived at by making A equal to 26; B, 25; and so on to Z, 1 (as in the top diagram on page 135).

The random five-digit keys in the center next come into play. Taking the numbers from the top page of the one-time pad, the agent writes one group of five figures under each of the numbers already used in the first stage. Of course, encoder and decoder have agreed in advance whether columns are to be read vertically or horizontally.

The third stage of encipherment is to add the two numbers together (also shown on page 135). These numbers are the ones actually transmitted.

The great advantage of the one-time system is that similar letters do not produce similar final numbers. The letter *s*, which appears four times in the above message, is variously enciphered as 50569, 38284, 62564, and 74862. As a result, the cryptanalyst is beaten from the start, because frequency counts are not possible.

Having enciphered his message the agent merely tears off the pages he has used and burns them. It is, of course, absolutely necessary to follow the sequence of pages in the book. If not, the person trying to decipher the message will be using a different sheet, which will be useless.

The Krogers' Codes

The major disadvantage of the one-time system is the amount of time it takes to encipher a message by means of one-time pads.

The Krogers had a good deal of time at their disposal, however. In the privacy of their home they could encipher messages into the early hours of the morning if they wished, and their burglary precautions reduced the chances of discovery. They transmitted messages by radio to Moscow on Tuesdays, Wednesdays, Fridays, and Saturdays. The sheer quantity of their messages indicates how busy their spy ring was.

The leader of their ring was Gordon Lonsdale, who posed as a Canadian businessman. The secrets they transmitted were obtained through two employees at the British Navy's Underwater Weapons Research Establishment in Portland on the English Channel.

The Krogers' cover was so effective that they might still be beaming messages to Moscow if the leader of their group had not broken one of the cardinal rules of espionage. Instead of using a *cutout* (a go-between in clandestine work) when he needed to contact the Krogers, Lonsdale made regular visits to the Krogers' suburban home. When he himself came under suspicion, he was followed there by the police on several occasions.

After careful groundwork, Scotland Yard sent Superintendent George Smith to visit the Krogers on January 7, 1961. Here is how he describes the important arrest:

"I knocked on the door shortly after 6:30 p.m. I knew Lonsdale arrived somewhere between 6:30 and a quarter to seven. It's doubtful whether we'd have succeeded in getting in with a jemmy [jimmy] as there was a Yale lock and a mortice lock on the door and two big bolts as well. I waited as the bolts were drawn back and the keys turned and then Kroger himself appeared. I told him we were police officers and I'd like to see him. I had one foot in the door, of course, just in case, but he invited us in and led the way to the lounge [living room]. Mrs Kroger wasn't there and I wanted to see her too. I could hear someone else in the house, and after a second or two she came in the room."

But Helen Kroger tried a ploy in an attempt to get rid of a small but vital piece of incriminating evidence. According to Superintendent Smith: "Mrs Kroger went into the bedroom accompanied by a policewoman. As she entered she gently closed the door and after a second or two I pushed it open just in time to hear her ask the policewoman to give her something. As the officer turned her back, I saw Mrs Kroger . . . bend down and take up something from a chair. She then faced me and came out into the hall and said, 'Oh, Superintendent, as we appear to be going away for a long time, have you any objection if I stoke the boiler fire?' And I said, 'Certainly not. But first of all, would you let me see what you've got in your handbag?' She wouldn't. So I took the bag and opened it up. Inside was a small white envelope and inside the envelope a single sheet of paper bearing a block of typed numbers."

It was an enciphered message ready for transmission to Moscow. Six one-time pads in scroll form were found in the base of a cigarette lighter in the Krogers' living room, and the cord used as an aerial was found in a wastepaper basket. But it took a thorough search over several days to locate the transmitter. The police used mine detectors. When they got to the kitchen, they removed the floor covering and found a trap door in the middle of the floor. It covered a hole about $3\frac{1}{2}$ feet deep, seemingly filled with rubble. On tapping around with hammers they discovered a small crack in the concrete, which gave them some leverage. After great difficulty they raised a four-inch-thick cement slab. Underneath, covered with a piece of wood and wrapped in a protective plastic covering, was the radio transmitter they had all been looking for. It was promptly nicknamed the "United Nations transmitter" because various parts of it had been assembled from many different countries.

The Krogers were defeated not by any weakness in their system, but by human errors of judgment. These will continue to dog the code-makers' world. No system, however electronically sophisticated, is proof against the human factor.

Above: a policeman emerges from the deep hole discovered in the Krogers' kitchen. Inside was the transmitter that was kept hidden and removed for use each time the Krogers sent messages to the Soviet Union. The trap door was made of a cement slab four inches thick.

The Voynich Manuscript

Yet, strangely, there is one exception, a document in code that has defied all attempts at analysis. What is more unusual is that it is not the product of modern expertise, but dates from medieval days when scholarship was limited and science was only in its embryonic stage. This extraordinary document was untitled when found, and is known as the Voynich Manuscript because it was discovered in this century by William Voynich, an American antiquarian book dealer.

The Voynich Manuscript measures about 6 inches by 9 inches in size and consists of some 204 pages. Most experts agree that another 28 pages are missing. It is written on vellum with a thick

Below: an illustrated folio from the Voynich Manuscript, a mysterious coded document that has caused great controversy among cryptanalysts. The manuscript has defied all efforts to decipher it since its discovery by an antiquarian book dealer in Italy in 1912. (Bodleian Library, MS Bodley 211 f 5.)

ink similar to printer's ink, and the illustrations are in color—dark red, yellow, blue, brown, and a vivid green. The largest number of drawings are botanical in nature. The writing flows as normal writing would, but on close examination does not form readable words in any known language. It is because of the quality of the vellum, the style of the calligraphy, and the pigments that modern experts date the manuscript as a work of the Middle Ages. Although one of the most carefully formulated arguments credits the Voynich Manuscript as the work of the 13th-century English Franciscan friar Roger Bacon, a group of experts in 1962 agreed that the probable date was near 1500. Bacon, a scholar and philosopher who was considered heretical by many, lived some 200 years before this date.

Voynich came across the baffling manuscript in the dusty storerooms of a Jesuit school in Italy in 1912. He bought it, along with the more identifiable works it lay among. Its whole history is surrounded with "if," "perhaps," and "could be," but seems to go something like this.

It was first specifically mentioned in 1666 in a letter from Joannes Marci, rector of the University of Prague, to Father Athanasius Kircher, an outstanding Jesuit scholar of the period who was also a cryptologist. Marci sent it to his former teacher as a token of his esteem after it had been bequeathed to him. Marci says in his letter that his benefactor had told him the manuscript had been bought at a high price for Emperor Rudolf II, whose interest in research of all kinds was widely known. It was Marci's benefactor who thought it might be the work of Roger Bacon.

How a secret Bacon manuscript could get to Rudolf in Prague is a matter for conjecture. One possibility is that it had been brought by Dr John Dee, the English scholar who was interested in the occult as well as the scientific. He visited the emperor from 1584 to 1588, probably as a spy for Queen Elizabeth, and the work could have come into his possession through one of his acquaintances among the nobles who looted the English monasteries after their dissolution by Henry VIII.

Once he had the manuscript in his possession, Voynich was determined that its long-held secrets should be disclosed. He sent copies to everyone he thought might be able to break the cipher, and to anyone who expressed an interest in attempting to do so. All who put their hand and mind to it—professional as well as amateur cryptanalysts—failed.

One of the biggest puzzles of the Voynich Manuscript is that the letters and illustrations are almost instantly recognizable. That they defy identification is the more frustrating. The only page of the manuscript with letters written in ordinary Latin script—the scholarly language of the Middle Ages—is the final page. It is only one sentence, reading: "Michiton oladabas multos te fecr cerc portas." It was this sentence that set Professor William R. Newbold of Pennsylvania University on the path of a translation that shook the scientific world in 1921. The sentence

Below: the English philosopher Roger Bacon and a pupil shown in a 15th-century Italian manuscript. Many students of the Voynich Manuscript ascribe its authorship to this 13th-century Franciscan monk who was known to have used secret writing—perhaps to hide his heretical views, some people believe.

MS. Bodley 211, f 5. Film Strip 168H 17

itself does not make sense. But Newbold was sure that Bacon had written the manuscript, and was aware that Bacon, when writing elsewhere about his seven different methods of secret writing, had referred to one in which the plaintext contained a large number of nulls—the symbols that mean nothing and are intended to confuse. On this basis he broke down the sentence into the Latin: *A mihi dabas multos portas*, which means "Thou hast given me many gates." "Gates" is known in cabalistic lore to be another word for "key," and Bacon was familiar with the Cabala. Newbold felt that this signified that the cipher went through at least two stages.

His next discovery was that the ink in each letter seemed to be composed of a series of dots, sweeps, and shadings. He was convinced that these were similar to a form of shorthand known to have been used by Bacon. Newbold translated these into a Roman script of 17 different letters. He then doubled each letter as it occurred in the shorthand he devised, and wrote them in a curious system of linked pairs. In this way the word *oritur* became *or-ri-it-tu-ur*. He then substituted each pair of letters with a single letter. Newbold never revealed either his reasoning behind the doubling of letters nor his key for substituting a single letter for these doubles.

The result of this was a Latin one-cipher alphabet that was gibberish. Newbold was not to be put off. He decided that the last stage in decipherment must involve anagrams, to which the drawings were clues.

What resulted was astounding. On deciphering a page illustrated with what appeared to be a spiral nebula, Newbold arrived at this wording: "In a concave mirror I saw a star in the form of a snail . . . between the navel of Pegasus, the girdle of Andromeda, and the head of Cassiopeia." He found out that this properly described the position of the Great Nebula in Andromeda. Could Roger Bacon have invented the telescope? He would have had to in order to make such an accurate astronomical observation.

Newbold's solution was quickly accepted by many eminent people, even if they did not totally understand the methods he had used. But within a short time he came under attack.

The first major onslaught came from a writer on the *Scientific American Monthly*. He pointed out that the linked letter pairs of *or-ri-it-tu-ur* could not be used in enciphering. He declared that Newbold had failed to show how letter pairs that interlock could be a method of putting something into cipher.

Newbold continued to work on the Voynich Manuscript until his death in 1926. Five years later came the most devastating attack on his solution. It was made by J. M. Manly, one of the best cryptanalysts in the United States.

Manly directed attention to the fact that the most important quality of any cipher text is clarity. A message written in cipher must not be open to interpretation; it has to be deciphered in the exact words intended by the encipherer. Newbold's failure

Above: the Andromeda Nebula, brightest spiral nebula in the sky. William R. Newbold, one decipherer of the Voynich Manuscript, claimed that the nebula was clearly described in the text, which he was sure Bacon had written. A telescope would have been need-ed, however, and there is no evidence that Bacon invented it.

Left: one of the Voynich Manu-script's astronomical drawings, identified as a spiral nebula. According to Newbold, the text referred specifically to the Great Andromeda Nebula itself.

lay in the anagraming stage he used for his solution. Any anagram has many correct translations. For example, the anagram ASELT could be *tales, slate, teals, steal, stale,* or *least.* Newbold, working with much more complicated anagrams than ASELT, could not have been positive that his proposed solution to any particular anagram was the exact one.

Manly also suggested that there were no shorthand symbols in the manuscript. He argued that the thick and thin strokes had come about through the natural decomposition of the ink. His final attack was on the grounds that Newbold's translations "contain assumptions and statements which could not have emanated from Bacon or any other 13th-century scholar." He felt that Newbold had been carried away by his own "intense enthusiasm and his learned and ingenious subconscious." The position of the Andromeda spiral nebula was discovered only in the 19th century, after several years of observation with powerful telescopes and electronic apparatus. Newbold, he said, must have stored that particular fragment of knowledge in some corner of his subconscious.

Another drawback to Newbold's suggested solution is that he could decipher only illustrated pages because he used the pictures themselves as the key. All the unillustrated pages of the manuscript refused to give up any trace of a solution to either Newbold or any of the others who tried to apply his system.

In 1945 a new conclusion was proposed by Dr Leonell C. Strong, a respected cancer research specialist and amateur cryptanalyst. He believed the manuscript was the work of Roger Ascham, an Elizabethan scholar who wrote on many varied subjects. Ascham was known to have compiled an herbal, which is a listing of medicinal plants and recipes for their use. Strong said that the Voynich Manuscript was simply an herbal, though a more ornate one than usual. Some experts agreed with him, but his theory is largely unproved and unaccepted.

In a controversy so thick with conjecture, it could be expected that sooner or later someone would come up with an entirely different concept of the Voynich Manuscript. And so it was. William F. Friedman, one of the most brilliant cryptanalysts of World War II, decided that it was not a cipher at all. Not long before his death in 1969, he declared that the Voynich Manuscript was an attempt to construct an artificial or universal language. He explained the drawings as being symbols of certain categories of knowledge, such as biology, botany, astrology, and so on. He based his idea on the fact that words and groups of words are repeated more often in the manuscript than in common language. This means that it is unlikely to be a cipher because all known cipher systems try to eliminate repetition rather than to intensify it.

The Voynich Manuscript today lies hidden away in the rare book vaults of the Yale University Library. It has never given up its secrets; but because cryptanalysts are among the most dogged puzzle solvers in the world, it may yet be solved one day.

Index

Picture Credits